Traci
Twentie
Family History

Stuart A. Raymond

FAMILY CENTURY BY CENTURY

103495205

Published by
The Federation of Family History Societies
(Publications) Ltd.,
Units 15-16, Chesham Industrial Centre
Oram Street, Bury
Lancashire BL9 6EN

in association with
S.A. & M.J. Raymond
P.O. Box 35, Exeter EX1 3YZ
Email: samjraymond.btopenworld.com
Http: www.samjraymond.btinternet.co.uk/igb/htm

ISBNs:
Federation of Family History Societies: 1 86006 176 1
S.A. & M.J. Raymond: 1-899668-35-7

First published 2003

Printed and bound by the Alden Group, Oxford OX2 0EF

Contents

Introduction

The sources available to the family historian researching in the twentieth century are extensive, but, with the exception of civil registration records and the 1901 census, little used. There has been little serious examination of twentieth century sources from the family historian's point of view. The only publication that I am aware of devoted solely to this topic is Eve McLoughlin's *Twentieth century sources.* Family historians may also find it useful to read the books cited below by Lord and Williams, although they are directed at local rather than family historians. The purpose of this book is to encourage you to go beyond the bare bones of the civil registers and census, and to work out your family's history, rather than just its genealogy.

One of the problems with twentieth century research is that access to many documents is restricted or closed for periods of between 30 and 100 years. We will not be able to consult the 1921 census, for example, until 2021. Closure of documents is often related to the fact that they contain personal information - which is usually the very reason why family historians need to consult them! Furthermore, many documents from the last few decades are still with the organizations that created them, and not yet publicly available. Hence conscription records from the second world war are not available; hospital patient's records are closed, as are the records of national insurance and family allowance; service records for soldiers from the 1920's onwards have not yet been deposited in the National Archives. Many records we know have been destroyed: for example, the survival rate for motor vehicle licence records is not good; virtually all personal income tax records have been destroyed. The location and content of some records has simply never been investigated by historians: what has happened to the registers used to administer second world war rationing? Where are the records of the bodies which administered school examinations? What archives are held by building societies? Have the records of estate agents or removal firms been deposited in record offices? Other records have only become available in recent years: the archives of the second world war national farm survey, for example, were virtually unknown to genealogists even ten years ago. It is likely that, in the next few years, many sources that have previously been unavailable will be released to the researcher. Rogers provides details of a variety of sources which are not available to the general public, and therefore not discussed here, but which may become available at some time in the future.

Twentieth century records offer the family historian an enormous amount of information. If civil registration records can be combined with electoral registers, trade directories, rate books and the 1901 census, much can be discovered. And there are numerous other sources to explore. Those discussed in this book are simply the ones which are best known and most accessible. There are many others to be found in record offices, business premises, schools, government offices, and in family homes.

This book is intended as a basic introduction to sources which are readily accessible. I have tried to identify web pages and books that provide more detailed guidance where they exist; mostly, full details are given at the end of each chapter. Unfortunately, more often than not, such works do not exist. There is nothing available to guide the researcher in using the voluminous records of petty sessions. Few general guides exist to guide us through the records generated by twentieth century licensing laws - which covered topics as diverse as grocers and theatres, taxis and pedlars. Planning records have not attracted the attention of any expert willing to describe them in print. Even the rate book has been left un-noticed by most family historians. There is much work to be done by those of us who have an interest in, and want to use, the historical records of the twentieth century.

This book is conceived as the first volume of a series which will describe, century by century, the records available to genealogists. As we proceed to draw up our family trees, we need to know where we would be likely to find information on our ancestors at particular dates. The purpose of this book will have been achieved if it enables you to identify a variety of different sources all throwing light on your family history in the twentieth century.

In writing this book, I have relied heavily on the books and web pages listed at the end of this introduction. On most subjects, I have checked what Herber, Hey and Fitzhugh have written. The holdings of the National Archives are described in detail on its web site, and also by Bevan. Anyone writing on genealogical sources is obliged to sit on the shoulders of giants, and we must all be grateful for the work of authors such as these. This book has been typed by Cynthia Hanson, and seen through the press by Bob Boyd. My thanks to them, to Exeter University Library, where much of my research has been done, and to my family for their support. I am also grateful to John Edwards, who explained to me the intricacies of modern record keeping by Church of England clergymen.

Further Reading

- McLAUGHLIN, EVE. *Twentieth century research.* Haddenham: Varneys Press, 2000.
- LORD, EVELYN. *Investigating the twentieth century: sources for local historians.* Stroud: Tempus Publishing, 1999.
- WILLIAMS, MICHAEL A. *Researching local history: the human journey.* Longman, 1996.

- HERBER, MARK D. *Ancestral trails: the complete guide to British genealogy and family history.* Stroud: Sutton Publishing / London: Society of Genealogists, 1997.
- HEY, DAVID. *The Oxford companion to local and family history.* Oxford University Press, 1996.
- FITZHUGH, TERRICK V.H. *The dictionary of genealogy.* 5th ed., revised by Susan Lumas. A & C Black, 1998.
- RAYMOND, STUART A. *Family history: a pocket dictionary.* F.F.H.S., 2003.
- BEVAN, AMANDA. *Tracing your ancestors in the Public Record Office.* 6th ed. Public Record Office 19. P.R.O., 2002.
- ROGERS COLIN D. *Tracing missing persons: an introduction to agencies, methods and sources in England & Wales.* 2nd ed. Manchester University Press, 1985.

Chapter 1

Sources of Information:
the Internet, Books, Libraries,
Record Offices, Family History Societies

Information about your family history may be found
in a wide variety of places - amongst old papers in the
home, in the minds of relatives (see chapter 2), in
graveyards, in the records to be found in church safes,
etc. But most written sources are likely to be found
in libraries and record offices. The internet is also
worth consulting; it will never replace books as a
source of information, but it does provide a great deal
of information for twentieth century researchers, and
is likely to be the first port of call for genealogists, if
only because it is available in most homes and is so
quick and easy to access. A detailed introduction to
internet resources is provided by Christian, and no
attempt will be made here to replicate his work. The
present author's *Family History on the Web* provides
a directory of the most important web sites, and is
complemented by the other volumes in his *F.F.H.S.
web directories* series: these are intended to be used
as you would use a telephone directory.

A vast number of web pages for genealogists are
currently available; by the time you read this there
will be many more. They offer:

- advice
- details of organisations such as family history societies, record offices and libraries (including many library catalogues)
- interests lists which enable you to make contact with others researching the same surname.
- databases, transcripts and indexes of original sources
- historical and genealogical information relating to particular families.

The advice offered on the web is usually fairly basic, and genealogical textbooks often provide much more information. The prime exception to this rule are the many leaflets on the National Archives site (**www.pro.gov.uk/leaflets/Riindex.asp**), which are authoritative on particular sources; for the twentieth century they provide essential information for tracing men who served in the forces, especially during World War I. Before visiting libraries, record offices, and societies you should always check their web-sites, which usually provide the most up-to-date information concerning their opening hours, holdings, and activities. Web-based interests lists, and sites for particular families, are normally unique to the internet. A wide variety of original sources have been transcribed and/or indexed on web pages; there are a sufficient number of birth, marriage and death registers, monumental inscriptions, and war memorials, for each of these categories to be the subject of a volume or two in Raymond's *F.F.H.S. web directories* series. Most of these pages are relatively small; however, a significant number of sizeable pages are provided by 'Family History Online', which hosts databases compiled by family history societies, including a number relating to the twentieth century. The most significant web-based database for the twentieth century is the '1901 Census Website', discussed in chapter 10.

The best on-line guide to web resources for British genealogy is the extensive *Genuki* site, which is the subject of Hawgood's useful guide book. The site provides over 20,000 pages of advice and information, including many transcripts and indexes of original sources. *Genuki* is complemented by *Cyndis List*, which is an online directory of web-sites (also available in book format). *Cyndis List* is international in scope, with far more North American content than British, but nevertheless should be consulted by all genealogists seeking web-sites on particular subjects.

Books (with CD's and microfiche) offer genealogists far more information then the internet, and in some cases, e.g. the Parliamentary papers, (see chapter 17) and trade directories (see chapter 13) are themselves primary sources of information; many of them have been reproduced on CD or microfiche. Many thousand books on twentieth century history have been published; those of direct relevance to the family historian may be identified by consulting the various volumes of Raymond's *British genealogical library guides.* The study of family history does require an understanding of the wider historical background, and it may be found useful to dip into Robbins' authoritative bibliography of British history in the twentieth century, in order to identify those books which are most likely to aid understanding on particular topics. Bibliographies are important: they should be one of the first ports of call for any enquiry, since they will tell you where to find the information you need.

Once you have identified the books that you need to consult, you will want to obtain copies of them. It may be worth purchasing those you are likely to consult repeatedly, such as bibliographies and hand-books. Any bookshop should be able to supply books which are in print. The publications of family history societies, as listed by Perkins (for microfiche) and Hampson (for books) are best purchased direct from publishers, or via GENfair (**www.genfair.com**) on the internet. Out of print books may be more difficult to obtain, but there are many sites on the internet which enable you to search the stock of hundreds of second-hand booksellers. You may be able to make contact via the web with someone able to look up a particular reference for you: a number of web-sites are devoted to look-ups. Virtually all published books are available in libraries, and most (unless they are rare) may be obtained, usually at a small cost, via inter-library loan through most public libraries.

Libraries are warehouses of books, periodicals and microfiche, and sometimes hold manuscript materials. A detailed discussion of their uses is provided by Raymond's *Using libraries*. Local studies libraries may be particularly useful, since they generally aim to maintain a comprehensive collection of everything published concerning the area they cover, and are able to offer specialist advice. The libraries and resources of family history societies are also important. They have created and hold innumerable indexes and transcripts of source material, which have sometimes also been deposited with both the local studies library and the Society of Genealogists (see above p.12, for databases on the internet). Many of these have been published, and are listed in both the county volumes of Raymond's *British genealogical library guides* series, and in the listings of Perkins and Hampson. The Society of Genealogists probably has the largest family history library in the United Kingdom, rivalled only by the British Library. University libraries frequently hold good collections of twentieth century British history which may be of use to the genealogist. The Guildhall Library in London has an extensive genealogical collection, including the publications of many family history societies; it also has one of the most extensive collections of trade directories in the country.

The use of libraries and the internet should always be prior to the use of record offices and archives. You need to know what you are looking for in the latter before you use them, and you need to know whether you actually need to use them at all - has the information you need been published? Books and bibliographies should enable you to find out. Do not rush to the archives first; if you do, you risk subjecting unique documents to unnecessary wear and tear; you also risk wasting time finding information you could have found much more easily in books.

Record offices are usually - but not always - quite distinct from libraries, since the management of books requires different procedures to the management of archives: unique documents require much more care than books, and preservation rather than consultation is the main priority. There are a wide variety of record offices. Virtually all county authorities run a county record office, which houses the records of local government, and also acts as a place of deposit for church registers, local business archives, school records, *etc.* The National Archives (formerly the Public Record Office) at Kew holds the archives of national government; it has, however, transferred census and probate records to the Family Records Centre, which it runs jointly with the Registrar General, and also holds indexes to the latter's civil registration records (see chapters 4, 9 & 10). The Public Record Office's recent change of name, incidentally, may lead to changes in some of the web page addresses cited in this book. You should, however, still be able to find those pages by using search engines to search the titles of relevant pages.

The web sites of many libraries and record offices are listed in the present author's *Family history on the web*. Library resources are listed on the *Familia* web site, *Archon* (on the Historical Manuscripts Commission's site) is the authoritative web-based listing of record office sites. The National Register of Archives (also on the H.M.C. site) holds some 43,000 unpublished lists of archival sources, which are indexed on its web site. A2A provides on-line access to the archive catalogues of innumerable record offices, and should be checked by all genealogists.

Many web-sites have been created by family history societies to provide information about their services and activities. Every family historian would be well-advised to join relevant societies. Well over 150 societies currently exist in England and Wales; most are members of the Federation of Family History Societies, and a full list appears on its web-site. The majority are concerned with research in particular places; there are also many one-name societies (which are mostly member societies of the Guild of One Name Studies - often referred to as the Goons), and a number with specialist interests such as the Quaker Family History Society and the Railway Ancestors Family History Society.

Virtually all societies publish a journal, which usually includes details of current events in the family history world, articles on their members research, and details of members interests (which may also be published separately). These interest lists are particularly useful, as they can lead to invaluable exchanges of information with other researchers. Most societies have their own library, and many are engaged in the transcription and indexing of monumental inscriptions and other sources. Some have extensive publishing programmes (details are given in the books by Hampson and Perkins). Regular meetings provide a means of meeting other researchers and learning about methods of research.

Web sites:

- Genuki
  www.genuki.org.uk

- Cyndis List
  www.cyndislist.com

- Family History Online
  www.familyhistoryonline.net
  Databases of family history societies

- The 1901 Census Website
  www.census.pro.gov.uk

- Familia: the UK and Ireland's Guide to Genealogical Resources on the Web
  www.familia.org.uk

- OBI-OPACS in Britain and Ireland
  www.niss.ac.uk/lis/obi/obi.html
  Lists on-line library catalogues

- Historical Manuscripts Commission
  www.hmc.gov.uk
  Includes the National Register of Archives, and
  Archon. Now a part of the National Archives

- A2A
  www.pro.gov.uk/archives.A2A/

- Public Record Office
  www.pro.gov.uk
  Now the National Archives

- Federation of Family History Societies
  www.ffhs.org.uk

Further Reading
Internet

- CHRISTIAN, PETER. *The Genealogists internet.* Public
  Record Office, 2001.
- RAYMOND, STUART A. *Family history on the web: an
  internet directory for England and Wales.* 2nd ed.
  F.F.H.S., 2002. New edition forthcoming.
- HAWGOOD, DAVID. *Genuki: UK and Ireland genealogy
  on internet.* David Hawgood/F.F.H.S., 2000.
- HOWELLS, CYNDI. *Cyndi's list: a comprehensive list
  of 70,000 genealogy sites on the Internet.* 2nd ed. 2
  vols. Baltimore: Genealogical Publishing Co., 2001. In
  early 2003, the website listed over 180,000 sites, and
  is expanding rapidly! New editions of the book are
  expected at regular intervals.

Books & Libraries

- RAYMOND, STUART A. *Using libraries: workshops for family historians.* F.F.H.S., 2001.
- RAYMOND, STUART A. *British genealogical library guides.* Many vols. F.F.H.S., 1988- . (formerly *British genealogical bibliographies*). Includes many volumes listing resources for particular counties.
- ROBBINS, KEITH. *Bibliography of British history 1914-1989.* Oxford: Clarendon Press, 1996.
- PERKINS, JOHN P. *Current publications on microfiche for member societies.* 5th ed. F.F.H.S., 2002. Also available on CD.
- HAMPSON, ELIZABETH. *Current publications by member societies.* 10th ed. F.F.H.S. 1999.
- COLE, JEAN, & CHURCH, ROSEMARY. *In and around record repositories in Great Britain and Ireland.* 4th ed. A.B.M. Publishing, 1998. Detailed list of both record offices and libraries.

Chapter 2

Aunty Agnes Says . . . :
Memories, Reminiscences and
Memorabilia

What inspired you to investigate your family history?
Was it the stories of Aunt Agnes about relatives long
gone? Was it the legend about an uncle who struck
gold in Ballarat? Or a story about 'money in
Chancery'? Whatever it was, there is a strong
likelihood that your interest has been at least
partially inspired by older relatives telling stories
about long-past family happenings. Or, perhaps,
refusing to tell you! Other people have inspired a
curiosity in you to find out more.

If that is so, then the obvious way to begin your
investigation is to talk to those relatives who first
inspired your interest. But not just to them. You
need the help of any relatives who can tell you more
about your family history. And, indeed, of anyone
who might have known particular family members
well.

Their evidence is vital. You can find out a great
deal from documentary sources, which will be dealt
with in subsequent chapters. But unless you
interview your relatives and family friends, you are

unlikely to discover much about the inner dynamics of your family before you were born. Who ran the family? Who made the decisions? How were children brought up? What were relationships within your family like? Which children were unable to marry the person of their choice? Who was forced into an unsuitable marriage, forced to follow a profession which they hated, forced to stay at home to look after a domineering relative? Who were the steady and reliable members of the family? Who were the drunkards? The ones who did everything right? And the ones who went off the rails? These are all questions which are unlikely to be answered by documents, unless you are fortunate enough to discover a detailed family diary. The answers to these questions may, however, be the most interesting things that elderly relatives can tell you.

You do, however, need to be prepared before you talk to them. Write down every thing that you already know about your family history. Obtain all the birth, marriage and death certificates that you can (see chapter 4). Draw up a family tree as far as you are able from the knowledge you have already. Collect all the memorabilia — photographs, funeral cards, family bibles, *etc.* — that comes your way. Have as much information at your fingertips as is possible before you go to interview elderly relatives. The more you know, the more likely it is that you will be able to elicit useful information. Take appropriate memorabilia with you — it may help to prompt memories. Know what questions you need answered. And make sure that you have a good tape recorder to record the interview. It needs to be capable of recording under any conditions, battery operated in case the mains is not available. Make sure that you have several hours of tape for recording. You need to be able to use the recorder as unobtrusively as possible. It is family information that you are seeking, not discussion about tape recorders.

Some of your relatives you will know very well indeed. Others you may have never met. Your approach to them will depend on how well you know them. It is always better to visit potential informants and interview them in person, rather than writing or phoning – or even e-mailing. But do let them know that you are coming: don't just drop in unannounced on people that you do not know. And be prepared to take time over the interview. It is not a task that can be rushed if you want every last drop of information that your relative has. On the other hand, you must not outstay your welcome, and need to be aware that the old and infirm may start to flag after talking for an hour or so.

It is almost certain that you have relatives that you do not know about – cousins to the nth degree. It may be useful to track them down and interview them. You may know that a relative had a large family in a particular place fifty years ago or more, and that contact has been lost. A letter to a local paper may find them, especially if you have an uncommon name.

Or you could try telephone directories or electoral registers (see below, chapters 13-14). A visit to the area might also produce useful information. It is possible that a distant relative may be trying to trace the same family tree. So always check family history society members, interests lists, the *Genealogical research directory* and web-based surname interest lists for other people researching the names you are interested in.

When you are interviewing your relatives, be aware that the quality of the information you obtain is dependent upon three factors – you, your relative, and the degree of communication that exists between you. Your role is to supply the questions, not to answer them! Don't talk too much. Don't cut off the flow of information by bringing your interviewee back to what you think is the point – you may cut off some important information, and you can always ask the question that has not been answered later. Remember that your own character is likely to influence what you are told. If you are viewed as an interfering busybody, you will get nowhere. If you are thought of as someone who is after the family inheritance, you will be treated with suspicion. You have to convince your relative that you have a genuine interest in the history of the family, that you are not after the family silver, but that you could provide a secure resting place for family memorabilia such as funeral cards or photos.

You do need a general idea of the questions you need

answered; some of them may be very specific. You need to fill in the information you already have — more names, more dates, places, and occupations. You need to know how your relative saw his or her family — their characters, their habits, their attitude to life. You need your interviewee to talk about the trivia of family life when he/she was young. It may help to prepare a list of questions that you would like to have answered — but this must be used flexibly, and not in a formal way. Informality is likely to produce much more useful information.

Your relatives are not documentary sources. Unlike memorial inscriptions or parish registers, they have the ability to work with you. But you must be respectful of their opinions, and be flexible in the way you approach your task. You must understand that some things may not be open to discussion: memories which are discreditable are likely to be quietly buried. You must be aware that even an outright lie is a form of communication. A good approach may be to get your relative to tell his/her life story; most people like to talk about themselves and they are likely to be happy to oblige. Judicious questions may produce useful answers. Family photographs may prompt more information about the people in them; other memorabilia may also lead to interesting reminiscences. Bear in mind that memories are selective. The information that you need to continue your research may have been forgotten, but anecdotes about your family that do not seem important to you may be provided in abundance. You need to record everything: what does not appear to be of importance now may subsequently be seen to be vital.

Once you have completed the interview, you should note on each cassette the name of the interviewee and the date, and should transcribe it, reproducing the actual speech as accurately as possible, without correcting the grammar, and including hesitation, repetition, exclamation and emphasis. You are then in a position to access its accuracy and value to your research. Do not assume that everything you have been told is correct. Memory sometimes plays funny games, and it is easy to be mistaken about the order of events, perhaps telescoping them, or getting the dates wrong. Your relative's account is also derived from his/her own memory of how he/she participated in events: it is necessarily a partial account, from one particular view-point. And it may exaggerate his or her role in the family – or it may repress painful memories. In other words, the facts always need to be checked against other sources, whether that means interviewing other relatives, or checking documentary sources for corroboration.

Further Reading:

- THOMPSON, PAUL. *The voice of the past: oral history.* 2nd ed. Oxford University Press, 1988.
- McLAUGHLIN, EVE. *Interviewing elderly relatives.* 3rd ed. Haddenham: Varneys Press, 1993.

- PERKS, ROBERT. *Oral history: talking about the past.* Helps for students of history, **94.** Rev. ed. Historical Association, 1995.
- HOWARTH, KEN. *Oral history.* Sutton Publishing, 1998.

Chapter 3

Newspapers

Newspapers as a source of family history share many characteristics with oral history. They may have a view on any subject you care to mention; they are opinionated; their factual content is not always to be relied upon. Their evidence must be carefully assessed for its veracity. Nevertheless, they do contain an enormous amount of information, and it is likely that most people have been mentioned in them at some time or other. The major problem for the family historian is to find the places where their ancestors are mentioned.

The first step is to identify the newspapers which covered the areas where your ancestors lived. This is best done by consulting the catalogue of the British Library's Newspaper Library at Colindale, which is available on the internet, and also in book format. This is the major national repository for newspapers; however, local studies libraries usually hold at least some runs of newspapers for their own area. A select union list of local newspapers prior to 1920 is provided by Gibson, et al. More comprehensive union lists are provided in the *Newsplan* reports, published by the British Library, which are part of a major project to preserve and microfilm newspapers. When you have identified the newspapers you wish to consult, you may find that you have to read it on microfilm.

The most useful feature of newspapers for family historians are the birth, marriage and death notices. Formal notices did, of course, have to be paid for, and hence those of humble means are unlikely to appear in such announcements. Obituaries, also usually concerned with the well-to-do, with people who were eminent or well-known, provide potted biographies of the deceased, and are likely to include dates of birth, family details, and discussion of the person's role in the social, political or religious groups with which he was associated. Accounts of funerals may be even more useful; they may include the names of all the mourners, sometimes with their relationship to the deceased, together with much other information. Such accounts are still to be read in the newspapers of some rural areas. When probate was granted, the value of the estate might be printed in both local and national newspapers. If a coroner's inquest was held, that too might be reported. Reports of weddings similarly often included details of the guests, and give details of the best man, parents, bridesmaids, pageboys, ushers, *etc.* Much more information used to be given than is usual today.

The information capable of being gleaned from newspapers is, however, much wider than just births, marriages and deaths. During the two world wars, newspapers regularly published lists of those killed or missing. The proceedings of courts of law were – and are – regularly reported, and if your ancestor became entangled with the arm of the law, the fact is likely to be reported in the local newspaper. Reports of accidents, disasters, bankruptcies, crime, civic celebrations, council proceedings, *etc., etc.,* are all likely to include people's names. If your ancestors were tradesmen, they may well have inserted advertisements in the press, and these too should be checked out.

The major problem facing those who need to use newspapers in historical research is the sheer bulk of the material available. To know that a needle is certainly to be found is no comfort when searching a hay-stack! If indexes are not available, it is probably best to identify specific events, with dates, that you wish to check. And be warned that it is easy to be distracted from your search by information that has nothing to do with your family!

Indexes to newspapers have been few and far between. Fortunately, a number of indexing projects have been commenced in recent years – although they tend to relate to the nineteenth rather than the twentieth century. The indexes to the *Times* are a particularly valuable resource, including references to obituaries, birth, marriage and death notices, inquests, court cases, *etc., etc.* These are widely available in reference libraries. Indexes to other newspapers are listed in Gibson, *et al.* The British Library's Newspaper Library keeps a record of newspaper indexes; inquiries may also be made of local studies libraries and family history societies. A few extracts from newspapers have also been reprinted in recent years; a good example is Janice Simon's *Marriage & obituary notices 1900,* which includes notices from the *Lynn Advertiser,* the *Wisbech Constitutional Gazette,* and the *Norfolk & Cambridgeshire Herald.* A very few extracts − again, mainly nineteenth-century − are available on the internet; it is likely that many more such web-pages will become available in the next few years.

Full text web-pages are also likely to become available in the future. Many newspapers already provide web-pages for current news; however, the only full-text publication currently on the internet likely to be of use for family history is the *London gazette.* This is the government's official publication, and carries notices on a wide variety of subjects − appointments in the civil service, the army and the church, awards of honours, bankrupts, changes of names, *etc., etc.* The web-site is fully searchable from 1900; a search on 'Smith' produced over 6000 results.

Web Pages:
- British Library Newspaper Library
  www.bl.uk/collections/newspaper.html

- Gazettes Online
  www.gazettes-online.co.uk
  Full text of the *London gazette*

Further Reading:

- CHAPMAN, COLIN R. *Using newspapers and periodicals.* F.F.H.S., 1993.
- GIBSON, JEREMY, LANGSTON, BRETT, & SMITH, BRENDA W. *Local newspapers 1750-1920, England and Wales, Channel Islands, Isle of Man: a select location list.* 2nd ed. F.F.H.S., 2002.
- COLLINS, AUDREY. *Using Colindale and other newspaper repositories.* Basic facts about ... series F.F.H.S., 2001.

Chapter 4

Civil Registration

The records of civil registration are the vital building blocks for anyone trying to construct a pedigree for their family since 1900. The information provided on birth, marriage and death certificates is likely to be the most useful official evidence that you will be able to find for your family history (although that is not to say that there are no errors in registration records!).

The information provided on certificates is as follows:

Birth Certificates
- the child's forename (or sex if no name had been chosen – the name might be added later)
- date of birth
- place of birth
- father's name, surname and occupation
- mother's name, maiden name, and any former surnames
- informant's name, address, and relationship to the child
- date of registration and name of registrar
- Registration District

Birth Certificates changed format on 1st April 1969; henceforth, the surname of the child was given (it had previously been assumed to be that of the father), together with the following additional information:

- places of birth of both parents
- mother's address
- informants address

Since 1947, it has been possible to obtain short birth certificates for administrative purposes. These are not of any use to the family historian, since they provide no details of parentage.

Marriage Certificates

- date and place
- whether by licence, after the reading of banns, or in the registry office
- names of the parties
- ages
- occupations
- marital status prior to the marriage
- addresses
- names and occupations of both fathers
- names of witnesses and officiating minister or registrar
- Registration District

The content of marriage certificates has not changed since 1837.

Death Certificates

- Name
- Sex
- Age
- Occupation
- Address
- Place of death
- Cause of death
- Name, address, and description of the informant
- Registration District
- Date of registration and registrar's name

Since 1st April 1969, additional information has been required:

- Date and place of birth
- Maiden surname if the deceased was a married woman.

The authoritativeness of the information provided on certificates is dependent on the knowledge and reliability of informants. There were many reasons why incorrect information might be given, why informants might seek to conceal true ages, embellish details of occupations, and give addresses which were not in fact the places of residence of the people concerned. Sometimes informants did not know the information required, e.g. the ages of the dead. A minor marrying might increase his age to avoid telling the registrar he / she needed parental consent. An older person might wish to conceal his true age – or might not know it. For the twentieth century information on the cause of death is more reliable, since that has had to be certified by a doctor since 1874.

Registrations were – and are – initially made by the registrars of particular registration districts. Copies of his entries are sent regularly to the Registrar General, who has them copied into his own registers, and indexed. However, the superintendent registrars of registration districts also maintain their own registers, and index birth, civil marriage, and death registrations. They do not usually index ecclesiastical marriages, since these are compiled in separate registers. It is usually, but not always, possible to consult these indexes, although you will still have to purchase certificates. These indexes are more authoritative than those of the G.R.O., since the process of copying has allowed more errors to creep into the latter. Superintendent registrars can supply certificates more cheaply than the G.R.O. – but only if the particular event took place in their district. Full details of the areas covered by registration districts are given by Langston, and also (prior to 1930) on the internet at **www.fhsc.org.uk/genuki/reg/**.

The Registrar General's indexes to births, marriages, and deaths, in separate series, are held by the Family Records Centre. These indexes have just become available on the internet at the *Family Research Link* website, where digital images of the original indexes can be consulted. From 1984 the information is in database format. Microfiche and microfilm copies of the indexes are also widely available in local studies libraries, Latter Day Saints Family History Centres, and some family history society libraries. Until the end of 1983, they were compiled quarterly; they are now compiled annually. They are in strict alphabetical order of surname and forename. The original volumes are heavy and awkward to handle; if this is likely to be a problem, it may be better to use the internet or microfiche. The Family Records Centre has a computerised index of births and deaths 1984-92, and marriages 1984-93.

The indexes provide you with the basic information needed to apply for certificates. Each index entry gives the name of the person, the surname of the mother in birth indexes (since 1911), spouses surnames in marriage indexes from 1912, ages at death (prior to 1969) in the death indexes, the name of the registration district, and volume and page numbers. All this information, plus the date of the index, is required in order to obtain a certificate. Unless you are applying to a district registry office, application must be made either at the Family Records Centre, or direct to the General Register Office, Smedley Hydro, Trafalgar Road, Southport, PR8 2HH. The original registers are held in Southport, not in the Family Records Centre. Technically, the General Register Office has been part of the Office of Population Census & Surveys since 1970.

There are many reasons why you might not immediately find the index entry you require.

Marriages were normally registered on the day they took place, but parents had 42 days to register a birth – so it might be in the next quarter's index. Some births were registered before a name had been chosen; these are indexed at the end of entries for particular surnames. The name that you are searching is not necessarily the name that is in the index: try different spellings of the surname. Is the forename a 'pet' name? Was the birth registered under the mother's maiden name? Remember that the index is based on a copy made by the General Register Office of a copy of the original entry made by the local registrar. No human copying is exempt from error, and here are four chances for error to creep in! Another possibility is that an event may have been registered by the army; there are separate indexes for them, as there are for events in the air and at sea. The Family Records Centre also hold various indexes of overseas births, marriages and deaths, e.g. those registered by British consuls or high commissioners.

It should be noted that civil registration in the Isle of Man and the Channel Islands was not the responsibility of the British government, and consequently their records are different to the English records.

Web Pages:
• Civil Registration in England and Wales
   www.genuki.org.uk/big/eng/civreg/

- England: Civil Registration
  www.genuki.org.uk/big/eng/CivilRegistration.html

- Registration Districts in England and Wales
  www.fhsc.org.uk/genuki/reg/

- Family Research Link
  www.1837online.com
  Civil Registration indexes.

- Ordering Birth Registration Certificates from
  England and Wales, using the Latter Day Saints
  Family History Center's resources
  www.oz.net/~markhow/ukbirths.htm

Further Reading:
- McLAUGHLIN, EVE. *Civil registration of births,
  marriages and deaths.* Rev. ed. Haddenham: Varneys
  Press, 2001.
- WOOD, TOM. *Civil registration.* An introduction to ...
  series. 2nd ed. F.F.H.S., 2000.
- COLWELL, STELLA. *The Family Records Centre: a
  user's guide.* 2nd ed. P.R.O. users guide **17.** Public
  Record Office, 2002.
- LANGSTON, BRETT. *A handbook to the civil
  registration districts of England and Wales.*
  Northwich: B. Langston, 2001.
- *Using birth, marriage and death records.* Pocket
  guide to family history. Public Record Office, 2000.

Chapter 5

Church of England Registers and other records

The advent of civil registration did not lead to the cessation of ecclesiastical registers of baptisms, marriages and burials. These continued to be kept to the present day, although the proportion of events recorded in them has declined greatly in comparison with previous centuries. They provide a valuable supplementary source of information for genealogists; indeed, consultation of them may obviate the need to obtain official registration certificates.

The Church of England has continued to maintain separate registers of baptisms, marriages and burials, in books printed for that purpose. Baptismal registers should record the date of baptism, the child's name, the names and abode of both parents, the occupation of the father, and the names of godparents. They may also indicate the date of birth; some also include the mother's maiden name. The relevant details were sometimes taken from birth certificates. If a child was legitimated by the marriage of parents after baptism, the register may be annotated accordingly. It was customary for there to be three god-parents, two of them of the same sex as the child, and one of the opposite sex. In the last decades of the century, it was possible to purchase ready-printed baptismal registers from the S.P.C.K. (who also supplied printed burial registers and confirmation registers). Prior to this, there was great variation. Baptismal cards were often given to parents, and should be sought out by family historians.

For marriages, the Registrar General supplies duplicate registers, which should have identical entries. One copy is retained by the parish, the other returned to the Registrar on completion. The incumbent is also required to make a quarterly return of marriages conducted to the Registrar.

The bride and groom had to sign both registers, and the marriage certificate that they retained. The bride signed in her maiden name, although she had already been married at that stage in the proceedings. The details included were identical to those required by civil registration.

A single register of burials was kept; a certificate of burials also had to be made to the registrar. Strictly speaking, the burial register should have only contained entries relating to burials in the local church or churchyard, although, in practice, funerals, memorial services, and even burials in other parishes, might be recorded. The record will normally include the name of the deceased, the date of burial (not of death) and the deceased's address. Until recently, no entries relating to the interment of cremated remains were required. A few parishes kept a separate cremation register.

Associated records may include bishop's transcripts, registers of confirmations and banns, and records of the issue of marriage licences. By 1900, bishop's transcripts of parish registers had almost ceased to be made – but not quite: a handful of parishes continued the practice into the twentieth century. The last bishop's transcript for Hawkhurst, Kent, for example, was for 1911.

Confirmation registers began to be kept in the twentieth century; they are now required by canon law, and record the names of those who confirmed their baptismal vows in the presence of the bishop.

Banns registers were required by canon law throughout the twentieth century, although not always kept; it is only in the twenty-first century that their use has been called into question. As in the case of marriage registers, banns registers are supplied by the Registrar General; the banns had to be read from the register on three successive Sundays, and indicated the names and parishes of the parties; the minister calling them was required to sign the register on each occasion. Researchers should bear in mind that the calling of banns merely indicated intention to marry; it does not necessarily follow that the marriage always took place.

It continued to be possible to circumvent the need for banns to be called by obtaining a marriage licence from a bishop. Records of licences continued to be kept as they had been in earlier centuries, and may have been deposited in diocesan record offices.

A wide variety of other records were generated by twentieth-century church life. Perhaps the most useful to the family historian are the church electoral rolls, which have been required in every parish since 1919. These should list all baptised lay persons who have applied to be enrolled; they must either reside in the parish, or have habitually attended public worship in the parish. The rolls were used to identify those entitled to participate in local church meetings, and to vote for parochial church council members, *etc.*

Other records might include P.C.C. minutes and accounts, parish log books, fabric records, registers of services, title deeds, parish magazines, *etc., etc.* All of these may contain information relating to ancestors who were active in church life. Parish magazines in particular may include notices of baptisms, marriages and burials. Unfortunately, much of this material may have been lost; even official documents such as electoral rolls and banns registers have frequently been destroyed. It is, however, unusual for twentieth century parish registers to go astray.

Recent parish records are likely to still be with parish incumbents or churchwardens, although some twentieth century records may have been deposited in county record offices. Records of marriage licences may still be with diocesan registrars, or may have been deposited in diocesan record offices. The county volumes of the *National index of parish registers* should indicate which registers have been deposited in record offices, and may provide some information on those still with incumbents. The deposit of registers is only required when the latest entry is over 100 years old; however, many more recent registers have been deposited.

Further Reading:

- *National index of parish registers.* Society of Genealogists, 1973-. Many general and county volumes, mainly concerned with earlier centuries, but listing some 20th century registers.

Chapter 6

Nonconformist Registers and Records

Nonconformist registers of the twentieth century may also be useful – if they can be found. Marriage registers ought to survive; since 1898, nonconformist ministers have been permitted to act as registrars, and henceforward their marriage registers conformed to the pattern already described for the Church of England. The Registration of Burials Act 1864 also had an impact on the keeping of registers: it required a separate burial register for each burial ground, including those of all denominations. But, apart from these requirements, there has been minimal control over the keeping of nonconformist registers. Many are still held by the respective churches, some have been deposited in county record offices, but many are either lost or were never kept. The county volumes of the *National index of parish registers* record those which have been deposited, but does not provide much information on twentieth century registers still in church hands.

There are variations in record keeping caused by the structure and theology of particular denominations. Baptists, for example, practice believers baptism; their baptismal registers, if kept, therefore record a significant moment in the life of the person baptised, but do not usually indicate dates of birth — which will have been many years previously. It is necessary to be aware of these variations when researching nonconformist records, and consequently a brief outline of the record-keeping practices of the major denominations is necessary here.

Presbyterians, Baptists, Congregationalists, and Quakers all originated in the political and religious upheavals of the seventeenth century English civil war. The Quakers — the Society of Friends — have kept detailed records of their members ever since. They did not practice baptism, but did record the births of children born to parents who were both in membership: a central digest was kept in London until 1959, although the number of entries recorded in the final decades was far fewer than the number of births announced in the *Friend*, the Society's magazine — despite the fact that the requirement that both parents should be in membership was increasingly ignored. Similar returns were made for marriages and deaths; the digest of deaths ceased in 1961, but the digest of marriages continues to the present day. These digests are held at the Library, Friend's House, 173-7, Euston Road, London NW1 2BJ. Records were also kept by Monthly Meetings, whose records may still be with them, or may be deposited in county record offices.

The other old nonconformist denominations had no central control to govern their record keeping. Many of their churches became Unitarian in the eighteenth century; in 1972 most of the remaining Presbyterians and Congregationalists joined with the much smaller Churches of Christ to form the United Reformed Church. Most Baptist churches are members of the Baptist Union. Their churches tended to view the advent of civil registration as a great victory for nonconformists, and did not see the point of maintaining their own records of births, marriages and deaths – although a handful of registers are listed in the county volumes of the *National index of parish registers,* and in the works by Ruston, Clifford and Breed listed below. Those registers which have been kept are likely to have been deposited in county record offices, or, if they are still current, may still be held by church officers. Researchers should also check whether membership lists, cradle rolls, church magazines / notice sheets, minutes of church meetings, and any other records survive; these are all likely to yield information about people active in church life. The minutes of Congregationalist church meetings, for example, record requests for baptisms and marriages.

Similar sources are available for Methodist churches, but these were under tighter central control. At the beginning of the century there were several denominations – the United Methodists, the Methodist New Connexion, Bible Christians, Primitive Methodists, and Wesleyan Methodists. These came together in 1907 and 1932 to form what is now the

Methodist Church. Its records reflect the fact that the circuit, formed by a number of chapels, is the central feature of Methodist administration. Ministers were, and are, appointed by the Circuit, not by individual chapels. They had the responsibility for keeping and maintaining registers. Baptismal registers may relate to individual chapels, or to the entire circuit; each chapel which has chosen to be registered for marriages has its own marriage register as described in the previous chapter. There may also be burial registers where chapels have their own cemeteries. Other records which may have survived include:

- circuit plans, showing preaching arrangements, with the names of preachers and church officers
- class books, listing members
- circuit and chapel minutes, likely to give many names of those active in church life

The records of Methodist circuits and chapels are normally either deposited in county record offices, or are still in the hands of local ministers. Many other Methodist records, however, are held in the Methodist Archives and Research Centre at the John Rylands University Library of Manchester, Deansgate, Manchester M3 3EH. This holds both books and archival materials; the archives include not only the records of the Methodist Conference and its sub-committees, but also the personal papers of over 4,000 people who have been active in the church. Amongst its books are many Methodist magazines and newspapers, which include innumerable obituaries of both ministers and laymen; some of these may also be available in other libraries. The Centre's website includes a 'biographical index', and provides details of various published lists of ministers *etc.,* as well as a number of published school registers.

The Salvation Army was founded in the late nineteenth century, and its administration is centralized. Records of officers, i.e. full-time workers are held on 'officer's career cards' at the Salvation Army's International Heritage Centre, 117-21, Judd Street, King's Cross, London, WC1H 9NN, although many of these cards were lost in the second world war. They may also be traced through the Army's magazines, the *War Cry,* and *The Officer;* indexes to these are currently being prepared.

'Soldiers' are the ordinary members of the Army. Records relating to them are maintained by local corps, rather than H.Q. The 'dedication, marriage and promotion to glory registers' is the Army equivalent of birth, marriage and death registers. The 'soldiers roll' records details of membership. And a 'transfer note' is issued and recorded when a soldier transfers to another corps. It may not be possible to see these records, but information from them may be available from corps officers.

The Salvation Army is known for its social work, and some records of its activities in this field are available at the International Heritage Centre. In particular, the 'girls statement books' provide details of children who were cared for in its homes. Wiggins has a detailed list of other records available.

Web Pages

Methodists

- Methodist Archives and Research Centre
  rylibweb.man.ac.uk/datal/dg/text/method.html

Quakers

- Library Guide 2: Genealogical Sources
  www.quaker.org.uk/library/guides/libgenea.html

- Quaker Family History Society
  www.qfhs.co.uk

Salvation Army

- The Salvation Army Heritage Centre
  wwwl.salvationarmy.org/heritage/nsf

Further Reading

- STEEL, D.J. *Sources for nonconformist genealogy and family history.* National Index of Parish Registers 2. Society of Genealogists, 1973. Still the standard work, but not very detailed for the twentieth century.

Baptists

- BREED, GEOFFREY R. *My ancestors were Baptists.* 4th ed. Society of Genealogists, 2002.

Congregationalists

- CLIFFORD, DAVID J.H. *My ancestors were Congregationalists in England and Wales: how can I find out more about them?* 2nd ed. Society of Genealogists, 1997.

Methodists

- LEARY, WILLIAM. *My ancestors were Methodists: how can I find out more about them?* Rev. ed. Society of Genealogists, 1999.

- *Who's who in Methodism 1933: an encyclopaedia of the personnel and departments, ministerial and lay, in the united church of Methodism.* Methodist Times and Leader, 1933.

Presbyterians / Unitarians

- RUSTON, ALAN. *My ancestors were English Presbyterians and Unitarians: how can I find out more about them?* 2nd ed. Society of Genealogists, 2001.

Quakers

- MILLIGAN, EDWARD H., & THOMAS, MALCOLM J. *My ancestors were Quakers: how can I find out more about them?* 2nd ed. Society of Genealogists, 1999.

Salvation Army

- WIGGINS, RAY. *My ancestors were in the Salvation Army: how can I find out more about them?* 2nd ed. Society of Genealogists, 1999.

Chapter 7

Monumental Inscriptions

Parish churches, churchyards, and cemeteries are full of memorial stones commemorating the dead. The major proportion of these relate to the twentieth century; many contain more details of the deceased than is contained in the burial register. Some memorials record whole families, giving extensive detail of relationships. There may be a plan showing where burials have taken place, but this is not always the case.

The condition of memorial stones vary tremendously. Some are well looked after; other have been allowed to deteriorate or have been vandalised. Some stones have been removed to make way for re-development, or so that the grass can be cut more easily! Some are now illegible. Consequently, many family history societies and others have undertaken extensive work in transcribing inscriptions in their area. This process is still continuing. Such transcripts are frequently made in triplicate, so that copies can be held by the relevant family history society, the local studies library, and the Society of Genealogists. The latter has an extensive collection from throughout the country.

In recent years, efforts have been made to computerise the transcription of inscriptions. Many family history societies now hold inscription databases; numerous individuals have created monumental inscriptions web pages. They are listed in the present author's *Monumental inscriptions on the web*. Family history societies (and others) have also published numerous transcripts on microfiche and in book format; no doubt many will be issued on CD in the next few years. Published monumental inscriptions are listed in the county volumes of the present author's *British genealogical library guides* and also in John Perkins *Current publications on microfiche*. 5th ed. F.F.H.S., 2002.

Further Reading
- COLLINS, L. *Monumental inscriptions in the Library of the Society of Genealogists.* 2 vols. Society of Genealogists, 1984-7.
- RAYMOND, STUART A. *Monumental inscriptions on the web: a directory.* F.F.H.S.., 2002

Chapter 8

Divorce

Divorce was much more common in the late twentieth century than it had been before 1950; if you are researching very recent family history, you are quite likely to need to check divorce records. Adultery was the only grounds for divorce in 1900; this was broadened to include desertion, cruelty, unsoundness of mind, *etc.,* in 1937; the Divorce Reform Act of 1969 made the irretrievable breakdown of the marriage the sole grounds for divorce.

The Probate, Divorce and Admiralty Division of the Supreme Court of Judicature heard all divorce cases in London at the beginning of the century. Local facilities were provided in a number of other places in the 1920's, and in the late 1960's the county courts were authorised to hear cases. There is a central index of decrees absolute, which can be searched for a (fairly high) fee; contact the Principal Registry of the Family Division, First Avenue House, 42-49, High Holborn, London WC1V 6NP. They will either issue you with a copy of the decree, or ask the relevant county court to do so.

The Principal Registry does not have information relating to decrees granted in other courts, apart from

the index. Records of county courts other than the
decree may still be with the courts themselves,
although case files are now destroyed after 20 years.

The National Archives does hold divorce case papers
from the Supreme Court. Prior to 1928, almost all case
papers survive; between 1928 and 1937 files from its
district registries have been destroyed; since 1938
most have been destroyed, although a very small
annual sample was retained. These are in J77,
indexed in J78. They are likely to include the petition,
copies of any relevant certificates, affidavits, and
copies of decrees; most other material has been
removed. There is a 30 year closure on these files.

It is also quite likely that there will be newspaper
reports of divorces, especially earlier in the century
when they were newsworthy; see chapter 3. There
may also be information on divorce to be found
amongst solicitors' papers, many of which have been
deposited in record offices.

Web Page:
- Divorce Records in England and Wales after 1858
  catalogue.pro.gov.uk/Leaflets/ri2289.htm

Further Reading:
- 'The central index of decrees absolute', *Genealogical
  services directory* 2000, 274.

Chapter 9

Wills

Wills were probably made more frequently in the twentieth century than was previously the case, but have been less studied by historians, despite the fact that they are much easier to locate. Most of us want to make provision for the disposal of our estates after death, for the maintainance of spouses, or the future of our children, for gifts to other members of the family, to friends, and to charities. Twentieth century wills disposed of both real (land) and personal (goods and chattels) estate; they name the executor(s) – formerly likely to be a close relative, but in recent times more likely to be a solicitor or bank – and sometimes trustees, as well as the legatees.

Wills were proved at either the Principal Probate Registry (now the Principal Registry of the Family Division), or at a district probate registry. Copies of wills that have been proved, and grants of administration, can be consulted for a fee, at the Probate Search Room, First Avenue House, 42-49 High Holborn, London WC1V 6NP; They can also be ordered by post, also for a fee, and if you have the date of death, from the Court Service, York Probate Sub-

Registry, First Floor, Castle Chambers, Clifford Street, York YO1 7EA. In older works these are sometimes referred to as Somerset House wills, since that is where they used to be housed.

The district probate registries retained copies of wills that they had proved, as well as sending copies to the Principal Probate Registry. These copies may still be held by the registries concerned, or they may have been transferred to county record offices; details are given by Gibson & Churchill. Copies of pre-1941 Welsh wills are held at the National Library of Wales.

All twentieth-century wills are indexed in the *National probate index,* which is now widely available, not only in probate registries, but also in local studies libraries, family history society libraries, record offices, and other institutions; in future, it will also be available on computer terminals at First Avenue House. The information in this index has varied over time. At the beginning of the twentieth century, it included the name and abode of the deceased, the date and place of death, the date and place of the grant of probate or administration, the name(s) and address(es) of executor(s) and the value of the estate. Occupations may also be given, as may the names of widowers. From 1958 the names of widowers were dropped; from 1968, only the name, address and date of death, together with the date and place of the grant, and the value of the estate are given. In order to order a copy of a will, you need the name, the date of the grant, and the name of the registry which made the grant. For London wills pre-1931, you also need the folio number, which is hand-written in the margin of the index.

If wills were disputed, it is possible that a pedigree may have been deposited in the National Archives, class J68; these are for disputes heard in the Chancery Division of the High Court since 1946, and are indexed by the name of the first person on them, the date of death, and the parties to the suit. A 7% sample of law suits to 1960 are in J121.

For a brief period at the beginning of the century, death duty registers may provide useful supplementary information on wills, although unfortunately they were discontinued after 1903. Indexes are available at both the Family Records Centre, and the National Archives (IR27); however the actual registers (IR26) are only available at the latter. These take three days to be produced. They show what actually happened to an estate, rather than what the will said should happen. They may also give a great deal of information on legatees and next of kin, such as marriage and death dates, addresses, *etc.*

Web Pages:

- Probate Records and Family History
  **www.courtservice.gov.uk/using__courts/wills__
    probate/probate__famhist.htm**

- Wills and Death Duty Records after 1858
  catalogue.pro.gov.uk/leaflets/ri2301.htm

- Probate Records from 1858
  **www.pro.gov.uk/research/leaflets/
  probatefrom1858.htm**

Further Reading

- GIBSON, JEREMY, & CHURCHILL, ELSE. *Probate jurisdictions: where to look for wills.* 5th ed. F.F.H.S., 2002.
- *Using wills.* Pocket guides to family history. Public Record Office, 2000.
- COLLINS, AUDREY. *Using wills after 1858, and First Avenue House.* Basic facts about ... series. F.F.H.S., 1998.
- McLAUGHLIN, EVE. *Modern wills from 1858.* 6th ed. Haddenham: Varneys Press, 2001.

Chapter 10

The Census

A census of population has been taken in the United Kingdom every ten years since 1801, except for 1941, when Britain was at war. Its aim was statistical; it did not occur to the bureaucrats that genealogists in the future would use it as one of their prime sources. Yet that is now the prime use of its records.

For the twentieth century, only the 1901 returns are currently available. Returns for 1911 and 1921 will not be open to public access until 100 years has elapsed since their compilation. The returns for 1931 were destroyed by fire during the second world war. No census was taken in 1941.

The 1901 census was taken on 31st March 1901. The census enumerators' schedules first give the names of civil and ecclesiastical parishes, local government authority and parliamentary constituency, *etc.* It then provides information in seventeen columns:

1. No. of schedule
2. Road, street &c., and no. or name of house
3-6. Houses (whether inhabited, uninhabited, or a building)
7. Number of rooms occupied if less than five.

8.   Name and surname of each person.
9.   Relationship to head of family.
10. Condition as to marriage
11-12. Age last birthday (divided by sex)
13. Profession or occupation.
14. Employer, worker, or own account.
15. If working at home.
16. Where born
17. If (i) deaf or dumb, (ii) blind, (iii) lunatic;
     (iv) imbecile, feeble-minded.

Some of these columns are obviously of more importance to genealogists than others.

The originals of these schedules are kept in books arranged topographically. However, normally, these manuscripts are not produced. Rather, the schedules must be consulted either on fiche, or via the internet. Fiche copies of the census schedules relating to their own areas are usually available in local studies libraries and / or county record offices; they are also available at the National Archives. There is a list of institutions holding fiche on the census website. In order to find information on fiche, you will need to know the specific place that you wish to search. You will have to identify the registration district in order to find the number of the fiche that contains the schedule you require. Institutions holding the fiche will show you how to use the indexes which enable you to do this. A full list of registration districts is given by Lumas.

Access via the internet is much easier. All 32,000,000 names have been indexed and can be searched by computer from anywhere in the world. It is possible to search by person or place; there are also separate indexes to vessels and institutions. Once you have found an index entry that you need to check, you must pay to view either a digitised image of the original return, or a transcript of the person's details.

Bear in mind that, like other sources, the potential for error in census schedules — and in the on-line indexes — is considerable. If you do not find the information you seek there are a variety of possible explanations. Indexers can easily mis-spell names. So can enumerators. Search the index for as many variant spellings as you can think of if you do not find the family you have searched for. If they are not at the address you expect to find them, search a wider area. Remember that houses could be numbered erratically, and that census schedules are not necessarily in house number order. Remember too that not everyone was at home on census night: they may be recorded in hotels, or staying with friends, in prison or on board ship.

Even when you find the right entry, bear in mind that the information given may be incorrect. The enumerator may have made mistakes such as mis-spelling names; ages may have been guessed; people did not necessarily know when they were born. There were also many reasons for lying about age. Equally people may not have known where they were born —

and the laws of settlement were still in force, requiring paupers to be removed to their home parish. Some may have feared that the answers given would be used to remove them, and hence lied.

The 1901 census provides a valuable base line for genealogical research in the twentieth century. You can use it to identify the members of particular families, discovering basic information such as their relationship to each other, their ages, and their places of birth. You can also use it to trace the distribution of family names, and hence pinpoint possible relationships which can be checked in earlier censuses and in other sources. Occupations are given, which means that you may be able to trace occupational sources (see chapter 11). Local historians will use it for detailed socio-economic studies of particular communities. The opportunities for research provided by the census are limitless.

Web Page:
- The 1901 Census Website
  www.census.pro.gov.uk

Further Reading:
- LUMAS, SUSAN. *Making use of the census.* 4th ed. P.R.O. readers guide 1. P.R.O., 2002.
- COLWELL, STELLA. *The Family Records Centre: a users guide.* 2nd ed. P.R.O. readers guide 17. P.R.O., 2002.
- McLAUGHLIN, EVE. *The 1901 census and how to tackle it.* Haddenham: Varneys Press, 2002.

Chapter 11

Earning a Living

The task of earning a living occupies a considerable amount of time even today. In the past, hours were even longer. Work was a major part of our ancestors' lives, and is consequently of considerable importance if we want to reach an understanding of how they lived. Fortunately, the records of employment – especially in the twentieth century – are extensive, although they may be difficult to trace.

Occupations are often referred to in records described elsewhere in this book – in civil registration records, the census, trade directories, sometimes on monumental inscriptions, and incidentally in many other sources. If you know what your ancestor did for a living, then you are able to pursue sources of information that might be available. Note the word 'might' – there are no guarantees!

There are at least three types of organisation which may have kept records of people employed in specific occupations: employers, professional and trade organizations, and the government, both central and local. The personnel records of employers often contain much valuable information: applications for jobs, records of appointments and service, apprenticeship records, establishment registers, lists of pensionable staff, *etc.* Job applications, where they survive, are likely to be particularly useful; they will probably give details of age, address, education, qualifications, previous employers, names of referees, *etc.,* and may suggest other sources which could be checked for further evidence. Other records are also likely to include dates of birth, addresses, and, more recently, information on bank accounts. Staff magazines and similar publications may contain details of internal staff movements; they may also include biographical notes on staff, especially at significant times such as appointment, retirement and death. Unfortunately, the survival rate of business and company records has not been great, and much has been lost. A few large employers, e.g. the Post Office, have their own record offices and employ archivists, but most business records, where they survive, will be found deposited in county record offices if they are not still held by the business. The records of government as an employer are somewhat better preserved, but – as with many twentieth century records – they may be subject to restricted public access. Current records are likely to be still with relevant departments and organizations; older records of the Civil Service, the armed forces and nationalized companies are likely to be in the National Archives. For example, a range of records concerning staff of the Ministry of Agriculture are in the National Archives, class MAF 39; this includes staff lists showing ranks and salaries to 1947, registers of service for established staff to 1929, and for temporary staff to 1920, and lists of staff serving with the forces for both world wars. Lists of established staff 1948-55 are in MAF184. For local government employees, the holdings of county record offices should be checked – although class MH9 at the National Archives has registers of the employees of the Poor Law Unions prior to 1921.

Professional and trade organizations also hold useful occupational records; their membership registers should enable you to trace the entire careers of their members. Frequently these registers will be published; for example, the *Library Association yearbook* has been published annually since 1891, and gives a full list of members, their addresses, and their employers. Similarly, the Institute of Chartered Accountants has published its *List of members* annually since 1896. Many professional bodies publish similar listings. Entry to most professions in the twentieth century was by examination, whether that was conducted by the professional body itself, or, more recently, by universities and colleges. Records of the examination results will have been retained; for example, the Royal College of Psychiatrists has lists of successful candidates in mental nursing examinations, giving names of the hospitals in which they were employed, from 1890 to the 1950's.

In some professions, the government has intervened

to ensure the maintainance of standards and for other reasons; it has sometimes required the publication of lists of persons qualified. In the merchant marine, for example, officers were required to have certificates of competency; consequently, the National Archives holds a list (originally on card, now on fiche) of masters, mates, engineers, and skippers for the period 1910-69 (class BT352). It also holds a register of seamen 1913-41 and various other related records. The medical professions have also been subject to strict regulation; the *Medical register,* published regularly from 1859 to the present day, lists all doctors, and is widely available in libraries; the 'roll of nurses' of the General Nursing Council is in the National Archives (DT11), which also has pass and fail lists for the Council's final examinations (DT28). Another example of the effect of governmental regulation is that companies desiring limited liability status (to protect shareholders from bearing responsibility for company debts) have had to register the names of their directors and shareholders with the Registrar of Companies, and to file accounts with him. Surviving companies' files are retained by the Registrar, whose address is Companies House, Crown Way, Cardiff, CF14 3UZ; there is also a search room at Companies House, 21, Bloomsbury Street, London, ECIY 1BB.

The government's *London gazette* contains much information on companies; it also publishes many lists of persons in various professions subject to government regulation, as well as lists of civil service and armed forces appointments, *etc.* Its full text is available on its website (see above p. 30)

Local government has also been involved in the regulation of occupations. Licences have been required to engage in a variety of different trades, and registers of licences issued may provide useful information. Taxis, for example, were strictly regulated throughout the century. Peddlars, gamekeepers (and other gun owners) and chimney sweeps required licences, as did inns, hotels and beerhouses. Gibson & Hunter's *Victuallers licences* (2nd ed. F.F.H.S., 1997), provides a detailed list of sources for the latter. Records of licences have been little used by genealogists, or, indeed, by any other historians, but nevertheless may provide useful information.

There are many other publications devoted to trades and professions; these should be checked before you pursue archival research, since they may provide detailed information on sources, or even serve as primary sources themselves. The present author's *Occupational sources for genealogists* and *Londoner's occupations* provide extensive lists of publications likely to be of use to genealogists.

These publications fall roughly into five categories: guides to sources written specifically for genealogists, archival guides, lists and indexes, lists of men and women in specific trades and professions, biographical dictionaries, and histories of particular occupations.

Books written specifically for genealogists are particularly useful, since they provide expert guidance through the archival maze. Books such as Sherman's *My ancestor was a policeman* (Society of Genealogists, 2000) and Richard's *Was your grandfather a railwayman?* (4th ed. F.F.H.S., 2002) are vital resources to all seeking ancestors in those occupations. Works such as these are similar to general guides to archives, but tend to be more focused on the specific needs of family historians. However, general guides are also useful: C.J.Edwards' *Railway records: a guide to sources* (Public Record Office, 2001) is solely concerned with the holdings of the National Archives, and has a useful chapter on staff records. J. Armstrong & S.Jones's *Business documents* (Mansell, 1987) has a number of chapters of interest to genealogists, including information on registers of directors and staff records. For those whose ancestors were involved in the brewing industry, L. Richmond & A.Lesley's *Brewing industry* (Manchester University Press, 1990) could usefully be consulted.

Lists of the names of people in particular occupations are frequently published. Members lists from professional organizations have already been discussed: their regular issue may enable you to trace addresses, employers, and careers *etc.* over time. Similar lists have frequently been published commercially. *Crockford's clerical directory,* for example, has been published annually since 1858; it complements the lists of clergy which are frequently published in diocesan yearbooks. Furniture makers are listed in *The furnishing trade encyclopaedia, who's who, diary and buyers guide,* published between 1936 and 1965. *Kelly's directory of the leather trades,* issued irregularly between 1871 and 1940, lists leather workers. There are many similar directories of specific occupations. General directories are also invaluable for identifying occupations; they are discussed in chapter 13.

Biographical dictionaries are another valuable source. If any of your ancestors were well-known in particular occupations, then you may find brief biographies by checking relevant biographical dictionaries. Many of these relate to specific trades. 5,000 biographies of artists, for example, are included in Waters' *Dictionary of British artists working 1900-1950.* The *Authors and writers who's who,* published irregularly since 1934, provides current biographies of many authors. *Who's who in the motor industry: a biographical dictionary* did the same for the motor trades between 1952 and 1972.

Histories of particular industries and occupations, or of particular firms, may also yield valuable information. They provide the background against which you must place the careers of family members; they may also yield clues to sources of potential value, and may even include biographical and genealogical information on the founders of particular businesses. The bibliographies of Goodall and Zarach should both be consulted in order to identify company histories.

Further Reading

- RAYMOND, STUART A. *Occupational sources for genealogists.* 2nd ed. F.F.H.S., 1996.
- RAYMOND, STUART A. *Londoners occupations: a genealogical guide.* 2nd ed. F.F.H.S. 2001. Further volumes cover Surrey/Sussex and Yorkshire.
- GOODALL, FRANCIS. *A bibliography of British business histories.* Aldershot: Gower, 1987.
- ZARACH, STEPHANIE. *Debretts bibliography of British business history.* Macmillan, 1986.

Chapter 12

Army Ancestry

It is not the intention of this book to provide detailed guidance to sources for the study of particular occupations. However, virtually every English family had members who served in the army during the major conflicts of the twentieth century, and especially during the first world war; over 9,000,000 men enlisted in the armed forces between 1914 and 1918, mostly in the army. Since army records are likely to be of importance for all genealogists researching twentieth-century ancestry, it is appropriate to provide a brief description here.

Most surviving World War I army records are now in the National Archives, and are described in the first two books by Holding listed below. The third title by this author, *Locations of British army records,* provides a guide to records which are in other repositories. Unfortunately, many records were lost in the Blitz. The most important sources now available are the records of service for officers, and for other ranks. There are files for 217,000 officers in the National Archives, mainly consisting of correspondence; most of the forms which detailed officers' backgrounds, and confidential reports on them, have been lost. The first step in tracing information about an officer is to consult the printed *Army list*, using the monthly editions to identify the dates of commissions and the units in which they served. The quarterly and half-yearly editions only list those holding permanent commissions, but do give additional information, including dates of birth and brief details of war services. Runs of the *Army list* are widely available in major reference libraries, as are the lists of *Officers died in the Great War* which should also be consulted if appropriate. Once these have been checked, service records can be examined. These are divided into several classes, but the majority, relating mainly to officers who held commissions for the duration of the war only, are in class WO339, and indexed in WO338. Other classes relate to officers of the Territorial Army (WO374), Royal Engineers (WO25), the Militia (WO68), and various others; full details are given in W.Spencer's *Army service records of the First World War* (Public Record Office, 2001).

The records of service for 'other ranks' are far more extensive, although many have been lost or damaged. There are no published lists of other ranks apart from the extensive *Soldiers died in the Great War* – so you are more reliant on National Archives records. The 'burnt records' (WO363) relate to men who completed their service between 1914 and 1920. These are only available on microfilm, and are in semi-alphabetic order; i.e. each film contains names beginning with a particular letter, but within each film there is not necessarily any order. Consultation of the catalogue for this class is therefore essential.

The 'unburnt records' in WO364 are records recovered from other government departments – mainly the Ministry of Pensions – and mainly relate to men discharged on health grounds. These records are in alphabetical order.

These records of the service of other ranks are far from being uniform in content: numerous different forms were in use. Originally, a record would have included an attestation form giving information provided at enlistment; if this is still present in the file, it give basic information such as age, place of birth, address, employer, *etc.* Discharge involved another set of forms, which would include a physical description. The 'Army Form B 103, Casualty Form – Active Service' was common to both officers and other ranks; if found, it will provide details of dates of enlistment, service details, promotions, transfers, leave, and anything else the bureaucracy might need to know.

The service records of officers who served after 1922, and of other ranks who served after 1920, are still held by the Ministry of Defence, and are not open to public inspection, although a precis can be obtained by the individual concerned or his next of kin. The address to write to is: Army Personnel Records, CS(R)2e, Bourne Avenue, Hayes, Middlesex, UB3 1RF. Far fewer men served in World War II than in 1914-18. The National Archives holds a computerized roll of honour listing those who died between 1st September 1939 and 31st December 1946. Burials are recorded on the Commonwealth War Graves Commission 'Debt of Honour' register (**www.cwgc.org**), which provides some personal details (and can also be consulted for deaths in other conflicts, including World War I).

Another source of information is provided by war memorials. These are now being recorded in the U.K. National Inventory of War Memorials by the Imperial War Museum. Many war memorial sites have been created on the internet; these are listed in the present author's *War memorials on the Web*. Transcripts of war memorials are often included in collections of monumental inscriptions (see chapter 7.)

War memorials often memorialize airmen and seamen as well as soldiers. So do the numerous medal rolls and citations held by the National Archives, some of which also include civilians. The award of medals for long service, good conduct, particular campaigns and gallantry produced a mass of documentation, as well as the actual medals themselves. Citations were published in the *London gazette* (see above, p. 30).

Many other records are also available, not just in the National Archives, but also in institutions such as the Imperial War Museum, other military and regimental museums and in county record offices, *etc.* Holding's *Locations* gives a detailed listing of resources in these institutions for the first world war. Other National Archives holdings include casualty returns, war diaries, records of court martials and of conscientious objectors, *etc., etc.*

Both world wars have been the subjects of many books. These provide the essential background information for studying the war-time careers of particular individuals. Many regimental and corps histories provide lists of officers and/or men, rolls of honour, muster rolls, *etc.,* and thus provide specific information for the family historian. Enser's two *Subject bibliographies,* and White's *Bibliography of regimental histories of the British army* provide details of what is available, although these are now somewhat out of date: much more has been written since they were published.

Web Pages

* Public Record Office leaflets
  www.catalogue.pro.gov.uk/Leaflets/Riindex.asp.
  Includes many pages relating to soldiers

* Commonwealth War Graves Commission
  www.cwgc.org/

* U.K. National Inventory of War Memorials
  www.iwm.org.uk/collections/ref_Aiwm.htm

Further Reading:

* FOWLER, SIMON, & SPENCER, WILLIAM. *Army records for family historians.* Public Record Office readers guide **2.** Public Record Office, 1998.

- HOLDING, NORMAN. *World War I army ancestry.* 3rd ed. F.F.H.S., 1997.
- HOLDING, NORMAN. *More sources of World War I army ancestry.* 3rd ed. F.F.H.S., 1998.
- HOLDING, NORMAN. *The location of British army records 1914-1918.* 4th ed. F.F.H.S. 1991.
- RAYMOND, STUART A. *War memorials on the web.* 2 vols. F.F.H.S., 2003.
- WATTS, MICHAEL J. *My ancestor was in the British army.* Society of Genealogists, 1995.
- *Using army records.* Pocket guides to family history. Public Record Office, 2000.
- ENSER, A.G.S. *A subject bibliography of the First World War: books in English, 1914-1957.* Aldershot: Gower, 1979.
- ENSER, A.G.S. *A subject bibliography of the Second World War: books in English 1939-1974.* Andre Deutsch, 1974. A supplement covers books published 1975-83.
- WHITE, ARTHUR S. *A bibliography of regimental histories of the British Army.* Society for Army Historical Research, 1965.

Chapter 13

Directories

For the first forty years of the twentieth century (excluding the war years) directories are one of the most useful and easily available sources for genealogists. Directory publishing was far more prolific in this period than it had been in the nineteenth century, or than it was to be after the second world war (although directories are available from these periods). The directory publishing industry was dominated by Kelly & Co., who set the standard, but there were many smaller publishers who issued volumes for their own localities.

The scope of directories varied widely. Some, such as the mammoth *Kelly's directory of the six home counties* covered wide regions. Others — far more than in the previous century — were devoted to towns such as Eastbourne or Bridlington. *Kelly's directory of Eastbourne, Hailsham and neighbourhood* is a typical example, having been issued annually between 1926 and 1940. But the directories most well known to family historians are those which cover single counties. e.g. *Kelly's directory of Hampshire and the Isle of Wight,* the eleventh edition of which was published in 1903. Sometimes, incidentally, the county parts of regional directories were also published as separate county volumes, and it is not always clear that this is the case – especially when, as is often the case, library copies have lost their title pages. In the preface to the volume just cited, it is described as *Kelly's directory of Hampshire (including the Isle of Wight), Wiltshire, Dorsetshire and the Channel Islands* – although the contents and title page only relate to Hampshire!

The content and format of most directories follows a common pattern. They generally have an entry for each parish. Most provide a brief historical and topographical account of the parish, including notes on topics such as the church, the post office, carriers, schools, etc., and the names of local office holders such as the rector, J.P's., poor law officers, registrars, postmasters, *etc.* This is followed by listings of 'private residents' and a 'commercial' listing. In towns and cities residents are likely to be listed street by street.

Sometimes names will be listed alphabetically, and then by trade. Indeed, in some directories, there are three separate sections, topographical, alphabetical and trade – and some names may appear in two, or even all three, sections.

Most directories were intended to be updated regularly, and many were. Kelly's local directories in particularly tended to be issued annually; their county directories came out every four or five years. However, smaller directory publishers were sometimes only able to issue one or two volumes: the 'Evening Post', based in Exeter, only published one issue of its *Dartmouth and Kingswear directory,* in 1908. It is worth seeking out such titles, even though they may be small; they may add something to the ubiquitous *Kelly's.*

Trade directories provide an easily accessible starting point for family history research. They provide basic information concerning names, addresses, and occupations. It is easy to use them to check a name, to identify the occupiers of particular properties, to trace the location of particular surnames, or to compare them with other sources such as electoral registers or the 1901 census. If a directory was published at frequent intervals, successive issues can be used to check when particular names first appeared, and when they disappeared.

Directories do, however, present problems for researchers. As with all original sources, an understanding of their original purpose, and of how they were created, is needed in order to use them effectively. Directories were primarily intended to enable tradesmen to identify potential customers, and to find their addresses. They were also used for similar purposes by magistrates, clergy, poor law officers, etc., for administrative purposes. The middle classes might use them to identify tradesmen; antiquarians and visitors might consult them to identify places worth visiting. Publishers used them to make a profit! Therefore, they did not include information that was not to their purpose. The typical directory entry for a village will include the names of the principal landowner(s), the farmers, the rector, and the more important tradesmen. These would be the people users would want to identify. It will not include the names of labourers or servants. And women are rarely mentioned. Directories are not censuses (although they are worth comparing with census information). They record the social structure of the middle and upper classes. Those at the bottom of the social hierarchy were excluded.

The problems caused to modern researchers by this exclusiveness is exacerbated by the fact that the coverage of directories is patchy. The rural population is not as well recorded as urban dwellers; such information was not considered necessary. Most men who were economically important were listed, but they did not necessarily constitute even a majority of rural households. Coverage in towns is usually more extensive, often including most households on the principal streets – although alleyways and side roads might be missed.

Problems may also be caused by the processes of compilation and publishing. The information required was usually obtained by agents visiting houses, or by asking householders to fill in circulars. That left plenty of room for error. Furthermore, compilation was a tedious process, which took a long time: most directories would have been six months out of date on publication, some much more — especially where they were reprinted from previous editions.

Over 2,200 directory titles — almost 18,000 volumes — are listed in Tipper and Shaw's *British directories*, the majority of them relating to the twentieth century. This volume also identifies the libraries which hold them. Full listings are also given in the county volumes of the present author's *British genealogical library guides.* Original directories will usually be found in the local studies libraries for the area covered. Major national collections are held by the British Library, the Society of Genealogists and the Guildhall Library; a catalogue of the Society's collection has been published, and the British Library's catalogue is available on the internet. Unfortunately, few provincial libraries hold collections more extensive than their own localities, although this is not true of the public libraries in Birmingham and Manchester. And few English directories are to be found in overseas libraries. Old directories are frequently found in second-hand bookshops, although if a particular volume is desired it may be difficult to find, and prices tend to be extortionate. A number of directories have been reprinted, but many more are now available on microfiche or CD; full listings are available in the present author's *British genealogical microfiche* and *British family history on CD.*

Many extracts from directories are also available on the internet: the Genuki site **www.genuki.org.uk** has many extracts on its parish pages. The University of

Leicester's *Digital Library of Historical Directories* includes the full text of an increasing number of directories which can be searched by name on-line.

Web Page:

- Digital Library of Historical Directories
  www.historicaldirectories.org

Further Reading:

- SHAW, GARETH, & TIPPER, ALISON. *British directories: a bibliography and guide to directories published in England and Wales (1850-1950) and Scotland (1773-1950).* Leicester University Press, 1989. The 2nd ed. published by Mansell in 1997 has no additional information.
- MILLS, DENNIS R. *Rural community history from trade directories.* Aldenham: Local Population Studies, 1981.

Chapter 14

Electoral Registers

Until the census returns of 1911 and 1921 become available, electoral registers will be the most comprehensive lists of inhabitants available to the family historian in the twentieth century; they become increasingly useful as the century progresses. They were first compiled in 1832, but by 1900 the franchise had been greatly extended, and that process continued even as late as 1969, when the age of voting was reduced from 21 to 18.

In 1900, the franchise was based on the 1884 Representation of the People Act. It had established a 'uniform household franchise and a uniform lodger franchise' common to both boroughs and counties. Entitlement to vote was based on the ownership or occupation of property worth over ten pounds *per annum,* and on twelve months residence for occupiers. University graduates also had the right to vote for their own M.P's. Most voters qualified by occupation rather than ownership, but land owners might be able to exercise their vote twice – where they resided, and where they owned land. Electoral registers were drawn up by poor law overseers in the counties, and town clerks in boroughs, and indicated how those listed were qualified. Sometimes there were separate lists for owners and occupiers. The arrangement of the lists could be alphabetical within polling districts, but this was gradually superseded by an arrangement in street order — which became normal after 1918, at least until the advent of computers enabled registers to be easily arranged by both methods.

It has been estimated that the 1884 act led to the registration of 60% of adult males. It was not until 1918 that the franchise was extended to all resident adult males, and that the property qualification was abolished; the residence qualification was reduced to 6 months. Women aged over 30 were also given the vote. Occupiers of business premises could still vote twice, as could university graduates. The 1918 act also provided for separate registers of servicemen. Absent voters lists' are important for identifying soldiers; they were first compiled from information received just prior to 18th August 1918, and issued thereafter at six-monthly intervals for a number of years. They give home addresses, regiment or corps, regimental number, rank, unit, *etc.* Further details are given in N. Holding's *More sources of World War I army ancestry* (F.F.H.S., 3rd ed.) pp.49-52.

Subsequent reforms gave women equality with men in 1928, abolished the business and graduate vote in 1948, and, finally, reduced the age for voting to 18 in 1969. All of these changes are reflected in electoral registers, which from 1918 were compiled by the clerks of county and borough councils, rather than the overseers. It is worth noting that certain people are still not entitled to vote: those left off the electoral register, for whatever reason, peers of the realm (they are represented in the House of Lords), aliens, lunatics and convicts. Until 1918, a number of other categories were also specifically excluded: election agents, paupers in receipt of public alms, postmasters and government revenue officers. Conscientious objectors also lost the franchise between 1918 and 1923.

Electoral registers have been compiled annually since 1832, except during the war years of 1916-17 and 1940-44. For 1919-26 and 1945-9 they were compiled at six-monthly intervals. Each register has three significant dates: the 'qualifying date', on which the elector had the status required for inclusion, the date on which the register came into force, and the date on which it expired. It is the qualifying date which is significant for genealogists: that is the date on which the voter can be definitively said to have been in residence, occupation or ownership at the place specified. Since 1929, the qualifying date has been 1st June, and the date of coming into force 15th October. In those 4½ months many changes could take place — removal, death, change of ownership, *etc.* — so it is important to make sure that you use the 'qualifying date'.

The prime use of electoral registers to genealogists is to establish the residence of ancestors. The fact that they were compiled annually means that it is possible to trace ancestral movements — the dates on which a family member first appeared in the register, and disappeared from it, are valuable clues in pursuing further enquiries. You should always try to compare the information in them with information drawn from other sources – trade directories, rate lists, the 1901 census, *etc.* Data on land ownership and occupation is also important. It may also be useful to use registers to trace the distribution of a particular surname; again, comparison with other sources may be illuminating. More recent registers, of course, provide an invaluable means of tracing people.

Electoral registers are normally held in county record offices and / or local studies libraries. Gibson and Rogers provide a detailed listing, although they do not include the extensive collection held by the British Library, nor those still held by electoral registration officers.

Further Reading:

- GIBSON, JEREMY, & ROGERS, COLIN. *Electoral registers since 1832, and burgess rolls.* 2nd ed. F.F.H.S., 1990
- SANDISON, A. 'Electoral rolls in genealogy', *Genealogists magazine* **22**(10), 1988, 378-80.

Chapter 15

Educational Records

Virtually everyone in twentieth century Britain passed through the educational system, and had experience at least of elementary schools (primary from 1944). Most of us have answered to school registers, many of us have sat examinations, some have been to university (although not as many as go today). All the educational establishments we passed through kept records of us. They did the same for our ancestors.

Educational records can be divided into three categories:

- records created by schools for administrative purposes
- records given to pupils and parents
- reports on school activities by outside bodies.

Most records kept by schools are likely to have been deposited in county record offices, or are still with the school. They might include admission registers, log books, staff registers, punishment books, *etc. etc.* Admission registers are particularly useful; they may provide dates of admission and leaving, ages, parents names, residences, and occupations, *etc.* Many registers of public schools have been published; there is a good collection of them at the Society of Genealogists, and its published catalogue may enable you to identify books that are likely to be held in other libraries as well. School log books record day to day events, and incidentally record the names of both pupils and teachers, giving details of sickness and other reasons for absence, punishments, successes, *etc.* There might be separate books for recording punishments, and for honours awarded to pupils. Some schools recorded the names of old boys who died in the two world wars on memorials; such memorials can still be seen sometimes. The names of pupils entered for external examinations might also be recorded in separate books.

Records given to pupils and parents might include reports, prizes, sports trophies, even the exercise books they used. Between 1901 and 1918 a standardized school leaving certificate was given to certain children. In more recent years, those who have passed G.C.E. and G.C.S.E. examinations have been awarded certificates. All of these documents and memorabilia may have been passed down through families and all are worth seeking out.

Reports by outside bodies are not generally as useful to the family historian. The Parliamentary papers (see chapter 17) contain many reports on education, but few containing the names of pupils and teachers. Directories (see chapter 13) are likely to record the names of teachers: see particularly the *Schoolmasters yearbook and directory,* which was published annually between 1903 and 1932. For boarding schools, the 1901 census (chapter 10) will record the names of pupils and staff present on census night.

The National Archives does hold many records of school inspection, but few of these will be of use to the family historian. Newspaper reports (see chapter 3) of school activities may be more useful; some even provided full lists of examination results. The records of examination boards, if they can be traced, may also provide evidence of examination successes (and failures!).

Many pupils sat examinations in order to enter universities. A few universities have published lists of their alumni, sometimes in their annual calendars – which should also be checked for university lecturers. Increasingly, university alumni officers are establishing web-sites which provide the names and – if they are still in contact – the addresses of ex-students. Most, if not all, universities have archive repositories which may hold information on former students. They never know when references or confirmations of awards may be required, and are consequently likely to keep permanent records of their students. If a detailed reference has been kept on file, it may be invaluable to the family historian.

Bear in mind that there have been many amalgamations and re-organisations in the higher education sector throughout the twentieth century. Many institutions may now be operating under different names to those they had 20 or 50 years ago.

Web Pages:

- Elementary (Primary) Schools
  catalogue.pro.gov.uk/Leaflets/ri2174.htm

- Education: Elementary and Secondary Schools
  catalogue.pro.gov.uk/Leaflets/ri2172.htm

Further Reading:

- CHAPMAN, COLIN R. *Using education records.* Basic facts about ... series. F.F.H.S., 1999.
- CHAPMAN, COLIN R. *The growth of British education and its records.* 2nd ed. Dursley: Lochin Publishing, 1992.
- *School, university and college registers in the Library of the Society of Genealogists.* Society of Genealogists, 1988.

Chapter 16

Courts, Criminal and Legal Records

The archives of courts of justice, the police, and prison authorities are capable of yielding a great deal of biographical information, concerning not only criminals, but also judges, J.P's., lawyers, victims, witnesses, policemen, *etc.* Many of their records may be closed to public access for terms between 30 and 75 years, but it is worth checking what may be available. The main focus in this chapter will be on criminals, but the wider context of the records shuld not be forgotten. Most of us have had some contact with police, and even such mundane activities as reporting an accident, or being burgled, may have resulted in our names and addresses entering police records. Civil actions have also left their mark in the records of quarter sessions, assizes and the Supreme Court.

  Particular crimes in the twentieth century enter the historical record in the 'record of crimes reported' book, kept at every police station. This included name and occupation of the person making the report, details of the crime, the value of any goods stolen, whether recovered, and whether offenders were apprehended and successfully prosecuted. This is complemented by the 'general report book', also kept by each station, and completed by the officer investigating the crime: it gives details of how each crime was investigated. When a suspect was charged, details of the charge was entered in the 'register of charges'. These records may have been deposited in county record offices, or may still be with the police force.

Until 1971, charges were initially made at petty or quarter sessions, who could refer cases to the assizes. In 1971 the judicial system underwent a major overhaul; these institutions were replaced by magistrates courts and crown courts. Most of the records of the latter are closed for 30 years, so cannot be described here.

Each case before quarter sessions involved many documents: the indictment, depositions and lists of witnesses, letters from prisoners in mitigation, the sentencing order, *etc; etc.* The clerk of the court required lists of justices and jurors for each session; he had to keep calendars of indictments, calendars of prisoners, a letter book, an order book, and a variety of other documents. These records are held by county record offices; a full listing of calendars of prisoners is printed by Hawkings.

The more serious cases were sent to the Assizes. Their records include crown and gaol books, indictments, and depositions, and are in the National Archives. Assize judges were assigned to specific circuits of counties, and the records are arranged accordingly. However, London was subject to the Central Criminal Court rather than the assizes, as were parts of Essex, Kent, and Surrey; its proceedings are to be found in printed format in the National Archives, class PCOM1; its archives are held by London Metropolitan Archives. Indictments to 1957 are in the National Archives, class CRIM4, indexed in CRIM5.

On conviction, calendars of prisoners, including names, ages, trades, details of offences, and dates, *etc;* at both Quarter Sessions and Assizes, were printed; these are in the National Archives, class HO140. After conviction, information about convicts will be found in prison records, which are most likely to be in county record offices, or still with the prison authorities. Some registers (to 1951) are, however, in PCOM2; there is also a national 'register of habitual prisoners' in this class, giving details of released prisoners who were thought likely to re-offend; these end in 1940 (although closed for 74 years), and copies may also be found in county record offices. A similar register of habitual drunkards for 1903-14 is at MEPO6/77-88.

After 1907, appeals from the decisions of Assizes lay to the Court of Criminal Appeal. Its registers are in J81; some case files, mainly from 1956, are in J82. Records of Home Office pardons and reprieves (to 1960) are in HO188.

The Court of Criminal Appeal is a division of the Supreme Court of Judicature. The other divisions of this court dealt primarily with civil matters; their records are a prime source for twentieth century history, and contain much of interest to family historians. Divorce proceedings have already been discussed, as have the probate records of the Family Division. Other matters dealt with by the court included bankruptcy, adoption, defamation, property disputes, *etc; etc.* Common law pleadings in the Chancery Division to 1942 are in J54; affidavits to 1945 in J4, depositions to 1925 and 1960-63 in J17. A variety of other records are also available.

Web Pages:

* Assizes: Criminal Trials
  catalogue.pro.gov.uk/Leaflets/ri2231.htm

* Sources for Convicts and Prisoners 1100-1986
  catalogue.pro.gov.uk/Leaflets/ri2195.htm

* Old Bailey and the Central Criminal Courts: Criminal Trials
  catalogue.pro.gov.uk/Leaflets/ri2245.htm

Further Reading:

* HAWKINGS, DAVID T. *Criminal ancestors: a guide to historical criminal records in England and Wales.* Stroud: Sutton Publishing, 1992.
* CALE, MICHELLE. *Law and society: an introduction to sources for criminal and legal history from 1800.* Public Record Office readers guide 14. 1996.
* PALEY, R. *Using criminal records.* Public Record Office, 2001.
* GIBSON, J.S.W. *Quarter sessions records for family historians: a select list.* 4th ed. F.F.H.S., 1995.

Chapter 17

Government Publications

How many people realise that the government is responsible for issuing far more publications than any other publisher? How many genealogists realise that much information in these publications could be of use to them? Of course, the historical and genealogical publications of bodies such as the National Archives and the Historical Manuscripts Commission are well known: some of these are mentioned elsewhere in this book. But the contents of Parliamentary papers tends to be a closed book to most genealogists.

This is not surprising: they are not created for the purposes of genealogists and may be difficult to identify. They are not even mentioned in Heber's otherwise authoritative *Ancestral trails* (Sutton, 1997). Nevertheless, they may provide invaluable information, and most major libraries throughout the English speaking world have sets.

A cursory examination of the Parliamentary papers for the session 1961-2 reveals a wide range of invaluable information. They include a 184 page listing of aliens who took the oath of allegiance in 1961 and became British subjects. The *Aliens and British protected persons (naturalization)* returns were regularly published, and should be consulted by anyone with alien ancestry. The *Report of the Medical Research Council* gives the names of its members, members of its boards, members in the research groups it supported, and the names of authors of research papers it sponsored. The personal name index has 31 pages. The publication, *Public boards: list of members of public boards of a commercial character as at 1st November 1961* is briefer, at 20 pages, but still could be useful. The names of senior staff and of the governing bodies of Quangos are often given in annual reports, e.g. the *Report of the Southern Gas Consultative Council* for 1961/2 lists members of its divisional committees, with addresses; the *Report of the Commissioner of Police of the Metropolis* for 1961 lists changes in senior personnel. Chief officer appointments are noted in the *Report of Her Majesty's Chief Inspector of Fire Services* for 1961; the report also lists the names of those firemen awarded honours by the Queen.

In order to use Parliamentary papers, you will need to consult their indexes. Close attention should be paid to the introductions to these indexes, in order to understand the way in which the papers are arranged.

Web Pages:
- Printed Parliamentary Papers
  catalogue.pro.gov.uk/Leaflets/ri2114.htm

Index:
- *General index to the bills, reports and papers printed by order of the House of Commons, and to the reports and papers presented by command 1900 to 1948-49.* H.M.S.O., 1960. Continued to 1979 in 3 further volumes.

Chapter 18

Tax Records

Many taxes were levied in the twentieth century, but few have left records likely to be of use to genealogists. Even the ubiquitous income tax has left no official records providing information on individuals – although it is possible that the records of accountants, solicitors, and banks, if deposited in record offices, may include tax records relating to their clients. Death duty registers have already been discussed – but even these cease to be available after 1903. The only twentieth century taxation records currently available to genealogists relate to the land tax, local rates, and motor vehicle licensing. The Lloyd George land valuation of 1910 was intended to form the base for new taxes, but will be discussed in the next chapter. Other licensing records are discussed in chapter 11.

Land Tax
The origins of the land tax go back to 1692; it was finally abolished in 1963. Returns were made annually, and include the names of proprietors, occupiers, and sums assessed. Survival of the returns for the twentieth century is patchy; a full listing of

what is available is provided by Gibson & Mills.
Returns are held by county record offices. It was
possible to redeem the land tax in return for a
commutation payment equivalent to 15 years tax; by
1900 many had taken this option, and their names
consequently disappeared from the assessments.
Commutation was made compulsory in 1949, leading
to an ever decreasing number of names in each
annual return. Nevertheless, if your family's property
had not been subject to commutation, it may be
possible to find their names in land tax assessments.
It may be particularly helpful if a run of assessments
can be checked, to date their first and their final
appearances in the record, which may indicate the
dates on which they entered and left a property (or
perhaps the date on which the tax was commuted).

Rate Books and Valuation Lists
Compulsory rating had its origins in the Poor Law Act
1601. By 1900, the rates were a major source of income
for local authorities; sometimes they were
hypothecated for specific purposes, such as poor relief,
water rates, lighting purposes, *etc.* Rate books
contain lists of householders and/or owners, with an
assessment of the value of their property, and the
amount to be collected from them. Valuation books
record the value of properties; they may record the
names of owners or occupiers as well, but not
necessarily so. They are, however, more likely to be
open to public access. Both types of record are

arranged by ward or parish, and then by street; they are rarely indexed, and have been little used by genealogists. They provide a useful source to compare with electoral registers and other lists of names. The rates were replaced by the poll tax in 1990, which was in its turn replaced by the council tax in 1993. Records may have been deposited in county record office, although it is possible that many have been destroyed.

Motor Vehicle Licences
The invention of the internal combustion engine resulted in a dramatic transformation of English life and landscape. It provided a degree of mobility which would have astonished previous generations, making it possible for people to live many miles away from their places of work, and enabling them to travel hundreds of miles in a day. It also led to bureaucracy and taxation. An early decision was made to institute a licence fee for all vehicles, and to licence drivers; the Motor Car Act 1903 established both. Many – although far from all – vehicle registration records survive; a list is given by Riden. Until the Vehicle and Driving Licences Act 1969, licensing was in the hands of local authorities, and most surviving records are in the hands of county record offices. Since then, the issuing of licences has been the responsibility of the Driver and Vehicle Licensing Centre, although there was a long transition period, lasting until 1978. The Centre does not hold older records.

Registers were kept in order of licence numbers, and give the owners' name and address, details of the car, and the date of registration. If you know the number of an ancestor's car, it may be possible to locate the relevant register. If you think it likely that an ancestor did have a car, it may not be too arduous a task to search the earliest registers to find the relevant entry. However, there are no indexes, so such a search would become impossibly tedious after the first decade or so of the century.

Unfortunately, no information on driving licence records seems to be available at present.

Further Reading:

- GIBSON, J.S.W., MEDLYCOOT, M., & MILLS, D., *Land and window tax assessments.* F.F.H.S., 1993.
- RIDEN, PHILIP. *How to trace the history of your car: a guide to motor vehicle registration records in the British Isles.* 2nd ed. Whitchurch: Merton Priory Press, 1998.

Chapter 19

Land Surveys

Lloyd George's Land Valuation, 1910

When Lloyd George introduced his famous People's Budget in 1910, he did not appreciate that he was creating a major archive for family and local historians. His proposals for a tax on land necessitated the valuation of all land in the U.K. – an enormous bureaucratic operation which created a mass of documentation. The Finance (1909-10) Act empowered the Commissioners of Inland Revenue to "cause a valuation to be made of all land in the United Kingdom showing separately the total value and the site value of the land, and, in the case of agricultural land the value of the land for agricultural purposes where that value is different from the site value. Each piece of land which is under separate occupation, and, if the owner so requires, any part of any land which is under separate occupation, shall be separately valued, and the value, shall be estimated as on the thirtieth day of April 1909". The Commissioners were further required to "record particulars of all valuations, apportionments, re-apportionments, and assessments made by them". The consequences of this requirement are the voluminous and invaluable records of the Valuation Office. The Lloyd George survey is the most comprehensive survey of land ownership, occupation and values that has ever been undertaken in Britain; consequently, it has considerable value for both genealogists and local historians.

The survey was commenced by compiling a valuation book for each income tax parish. This was based initially on the income tax 'schedule A' rate books, which provided brief descriptions of property, the names of landowners and occupiers and its rateable value. Information about property which had not been noted for 'schedule A' had to be sought by the responsible land valuation officer, and is usually entered at the end of the schedule A entries, usually in a different hand, and often with less information. Further information was added in the Valuation Office: map references, the extent of the property as determined from Ordnance Survey plans, comments, even street indexes. Amendments to the information provided were also frequently made. Valuation books are mostly in county record offices.

At the same time as the valuation books were being compiled, land-owners were required to render a return on 'form 4 − land' giving details of their land-holdings − its situation, description, value, and names of occupiers. Most of these forms have been destroyed, but they were collated with the valuation books in order to produce the field books, in which land valuations were actually made. There are 95,000 field books in the National Archives, class IR58. These books were used in the field, hence their name. In conjunction with an Ordnance Survey map, valuation assistants used them to assess the value of each property. These are the fullest and most useful of the documents resulting from the survey. Each 'hereditament', i.e. property had four pages devoted to it. The first was a copy of 'form 4 – land'. A full description of the property was given on the second page, together with notes made on inspection. These descriptions can be very detailed, including, for example, notes on land use, the condition of buildings, water supply, *etc.* Page 3 provides additional descriptive information, sometimes including sketch plans, or even photographs. The lower half of page 2, and page 4, are devoted to the calculation of values.

The next stage in the process was the issue of provisional valuations. These were compiled on form 37 – Land; which have sometimes been retained by county record offices. Again, these forms provide details of each property, with the names of occupiers. In some cases they were updated as recently as 1945. They are likely to be more accurate than the valuation books and field books, and are the only documents which can always be unambiguously linked, by virtue of the hereditament numbers recorded on them, to the record sheet plans which were compiled from Ordnance Survey maps (mainly 1:2500), and which map each property. These plans are in the National Archives, classes IR121 and IR124-135. The original rough drafts of these plans are in county record offices.

In the process of transferring this huge archive from the Valuation Office to record offices, much material was lost: however, a great deal of valuable information still survives. For family historians, the documents provide very full details of owners and occupiers names and addresses, and the land they held. They enable us to see inside our ancestors' houses, to examine their construction, their condition, and their value, to discover the conditions in which our ancestors lived. They provide detailed description of land use, throwing some light on how our ancestors farmed, sometimes even on a field by field basis. If we had shop-keepers amongst our ancestors, their shops may be described in detail. If our aim as family historians is to reach an appreciation of the lives of our ancestors and the conditions in which they lived, then the work of Lloyd George has produced – quite unintentionally from his point of view – a major source of information.

The National Farm Survey 1941-3

The national farm survey of 1941-3 is another major source at the National Archives which may be of use to family historians, especially in view of the fact that no census was taken in 1941 (even if it had been, it would not be available for many years). The survey was not as comprehensive as the Lloyd George valuation: it only covered agricultural land. But it can be used to identify all owners and tenants of farms.

The survey was occasioned by the outbreak of war in 1939, which cut Britain off from its overseas food supplies. There was an urgent need to increase food production, and to bring large areas of land back into cultivation. Consequently, the Minister of Agriculture and Fisheries was empowered to establish County War Agricultural Committees, with authority to increase food production. Their first task was to ensure that large areas of grass land were ploughed up for planting. In the process, they surveyed the productive capacity of every farm. Unfortunately, records of this survey do not survive, although there are address lists of farmers within each parish for June 1940 in MAF65.

Once the object of increasing production had been met, the government decided to implement a more far-reaching survey in order to provide data for long-term planning. This covered every agricultural holding of more than five acres, including market gardens, horticulturists, and poultry keepers. The survey began in 1941 and was completed by the end of 1943.

The records of this survey are held by the National Archives, class MAF32, and are arranged by county; there is a separate file for each parish. Associated maps are in class MAF73. The MAF32 file should contain four forms for each farm: three separate returns dated 4th June 1941 and completed by the farmer, giving (a) details of small fruit, vegetables and stacks of hay and straw, (b) details of crops and grass, livestock, and labour employed, (c) additional questions on labour, machine power, tractors, rent payable, and length of occupancy. In addition the 'primary survey', obtained by inspection and interview, covered tenure, conditions of the farm, water and electricity, management, general comments, and grass fields ploughed up. It also required an assessment of farmers' abilities. Inspectors had to decide whether farms were managed well (A), fairly (B) or badly (C). Reasons are given on the forms if (B) or (C) applied: these might include old age, lack of capital, personal failings such as drunkenness, *etc.*

The survey also required the compilation of maps of the boundaries and fields of each holding; these are in MAF73, and are based on Ordnance Survey 6 inch and 25 inch sheet maps. These maps provide valuable visual evidence of the conditions in which our fathers and grandfathers lived.

The MAF32 files may yield valuable information about family life. In particular, inspectors comments on the failings of particular farmers may be illuminating! Notes on length of tenancy, and on tenure, may also provide helpful clues to finding further information. Overall, each return provides interesting factual details of what it was like to live in rural areas during the early 1940's.

Web Pages:

- Valuation Office records: the Finance (1909-1910) Act
  catalogue.pro.gov.uk/Leaflets/ri2153.htm

- National Farm Surveys of England and Wales
  1940-1943
  catalogue.pro.gov.uk/Leaflets/ri2271.htm

Further Reading:

- SHORT, BRIAN D. 'The Lloyd George Finance Act
  material', in THOMPSON, K.M. *Short guides to records:
  Second series: Guides 25-48.* Historical Association,
  1997, 63-8.

- SHORT, BRIAN. *Land and society in Edwardian
  Britain.* Cambridge University Press, 1997.

- FOOT, WILLIAM. *Maps for family history: a guide to
  the records of the tithe, Valuation Office, and
  National Farm Surveys of England and Wales, 1836-
  1943.* P.R.O. readers guide **9.** P.R.O. Publications,
  1994.

Chapter 20

Immigration

England in 2000 was a much more cosmopolitan country than it had been a century earlier. In 1900, it would have been rare to meet anyone born overseas, except perhaps in London and a few other centres. Immigration was on a much smaller scale; the census enumerators counted a mere 286,952 aliens in 1901.

At the beginning of the twentieth century, there were no controls on immigration. That policy was changed by the Aliens Act 1905, which was intended to restrict the influx of Jewish refugees from Eastern Europe. The outbreak of war in 1914 led to tighter restrictions: the Aliens Registration Act 1914 required all aliens to register with the police. The British Nationality and Status of Aliens Act of 1914 had the opposite effect: it conferred the status of British subject on all inhabitants of the British Empire, a principle subsequently reinforced by the British Nationality Act 1948.

Immigration in the first half of the century was not huge, and was predominantly European in character: refugees from both world wars, prisoners of war who decided not to return to their home countries, economic migrants such as the Irish, *etc.* A number of small communities of non-Europeans did establish themselves in port cities such as London and Liverpool but by 1951 there were a mere 32,475 Asian born resident in England and Wales, compared with 524,950 Europeans. That has changed dramatically; the 1991 census revealed 1,662,619 residents born in the 'new commonwealth', compared to 650,784 Europeans.

There are a variety of sources which family historians can use to trace immigrant ancestors. The most accessible source are the returns of *Aliens and British protected persons (naturalization)*, printed annually in the Parliamentary papers (see chapter 17) until 1961. There are also naturalization certificates granted prior to 1961 in the National Archives, class HO334. These returns and certificates will not, of course, mention inhabitants of the British Empire who become British subjects in 1914. After 1948, however, such subjects could acquire a registration certificate, and have their status registered; records of these R certificates (as they are known) are held by the National Archives (HO334) (until 1987), but, if the certificate number is unknown, the inquirer must first write to the Immigration and Nationality Department, Liverpool Nationality Office, B4 Division, India Buildings, Water Street, Liverpool, L2 0QN to obtain it. These certificates provide the applicant's (and spouse's) name, address, date and place of birth, father's name, and nationality. Post-1969 certificates are available via the Home Office, Record Management

Services, 50, Queen Anne's Gate, London SW1 9AH, although there are restrictions on the provision of information if they are less than 30 years old. A variety of other records on the grant of naturalization *etc.* are listed by Kershaw and Pearsall.

Mention has already been made of the 1914 requirement that aliens must register with the police. Police registers of aliens may be found in county record offices, or may still be with police authorities; Kershaw and Pearsall provide a listing, although it is probably incomplete. These registers indicate names, addresses, marital status, and occupations (with employer's addresses); they include photographs.

Aliens who had any contact with the Home Office had their own files which would have been maintained from the initial application for employment or visa, until the grant of naturalization. The series of files was begun in 1934, but may contain older papers; they are currently in the process of transfer to the National Archives. They are mostly closed to public access; however, the Home Office will review the closure of individual files on request.

Passenger lists are another important source. The Merchant Shipping Act 1894 required lists of all passengers arriving in British ports on board merchant shipping. Lists for ships arriving from non-European ports only are in the National Archives, class BT26, and run to 1960. Unfortunately, however, there is no index to these lists; if you are to have any chance of finding a particular individual on them, you need to know the port and the approximate date of arrival.

Web Pages:

- Immigrants
  catalogue.pro.gov.uk/Leaflets/ri2157.htm

- Grants of British Nationality
  catalogue.pro.gov.uk/Leaflets/ri2156.htm

Further Reading:

- KERSHAW, ROGER, & PEARSALL, MARK. *Immigrants and aliens: a guide to sources on U.K. immigration and citizenship.* Public Record Office readers guide **22**. P.R.O., 2000.

Chapter 21

Emigration

Millions of people emigrated from Britain during the twentieth century, primarily for economic reasons. At the beginning of the century the U.S.A. was the most popular destination, chosen by 61% of emigrants. However, by 1910 51% were choosing the dominions – Canada, Australia and New Zealand – and these continued to be the main destinations for migrants for much of the century. By the 1990's, more British people were resident in the European Community than in Australia, which was the only one of the old dominions to attract more than 10,000 British immigrants per year, averaging 37,800 per year between 1988 and 1992.

Sources for tracing individual emigrants are extensive but scattered. Many sources are located in London; many more may be found in the countries to which they migrated.

The National Archives, the Family Records Centre, Lambeth Palace Library, and Guildhall Library, all hold many registers of births marriages and deaths overseas, originating from British consuls, army units posted overseas, English overseas churches, *etc.* These are listed by Yeo. Searches should also be made in similar registers held by archives in destination countries. Civil registration records of overseas countries may also be available, as may twentieth-century census returns.

The outward passenger lists of the Board of Trade, now in the National Archives (BT27) run from 1890 to 1960, and should, in theory, list everyone leaving the U.K. by ship for destinations outside of Europe. However, they are not indexed, and you need to know the port and date of departure in order to locate particular individuals.

Passenger lists are also found in many overseas repositories, and many thousands are available on the internet. Lists for all Australian ports (with some gaps) survive from 1924 in the National Archives of Australia; there are also some earlier lists. For New Zealand, lists are available for the whole century at Archives New Zealand. Canadian lists are held by the National Archives of Canada, and run to 1935. For the United States, immigration passenger lists are held by the National Archives and Records Administration. Some 22,000,000 arrivals at Ellis Island, New York between 1892 and 1924 are indexed on the Ellis Island website. The amount of information given on these lists varies, but usually includes name, age, occupation and nationality. United States lists also give last residence, and, if going to join a relative, the relative's name. From 1903, they also include a physical description, and passenger's birthplace.

Passport records also provide a useful source. Passports only became compulsory for overseas travel in 1915, although they were issued earlier. Registers of passports issued prior to 1948 are in the National Archives, class FO610. They are chronological, and show the name of the applicant, the date, and the number of the passport; they also indicate the applicant's proposed destination, and the name of the person recommending him. Indexes to 1916 are in FO611.

The U.K. Passport Office has records of passports issued since 1898, and will search its records for the passport holder or next-of-kin, but not for genealogical inquiries. The information provided includes passport number, date and place of issue, full name of the bearer, and place and date of birth. Their address is Discharge of Information Section, Aragon Court, Peterborough, PE1 1QG.

Passenger lists and passport records are the only sources likely to mention the great majority of British emigrants. There are, however, a multitude of sources relating to specific categories of emigrants. Only a few of these can be dealt with here. Kershaw's *Emigrants and expats* provides a useful overview of resources in the National Archives and elsewhere. Just as many records are held by the archive authorities of the countries where migrants settled.

There were many different reasons for emigration, and also for temporary residence overseas. Civil servants and army officers were required to govern the colonies, and sometimes stayed in them. The colonies also provided a convenient home for children who could not be cared for in the U.K. De-mobilized soldiers were offered a free passage to the colonies after the First World War. The English brides of de-mobilized North American servicemen crossed the Atlantic with them. Many other groups could be similarly identified.

Sources for army ancestry have already been discussed; the careers of those who were posted overseas can be traced through them. However, these sources are limited for officers of the Indian Army, which was staffed by British officers until 1947. Their careers may be traced through the published *Indian army lists.* The archives of the Indian Army are now held in the British Library's Oriental and India Office collections, although some records are in the National Archives.

Civil servants posted overseas are listed in the annual *British imperial calendar,* which became the *Civil service yearbook* in 1972. The *Foreign Office list* became the *Diplomatic Service list* from 1966; there is also the *Commonwealth Relations Office list* from 1953. All of these annual publications may be found in major reference libraries, and may be used to trace the careers of senior civil servants. However, such men are also likely to have been the subjects of entries in biographical dictionaries, which may be the best place to begin.

Children were another important group of emigrants. Prior to 1967, a number of organizations were involved in arranging their emigration. Their purpose was to increase the British population of the colonies, and to promote their economies; the wishes of the children themselves were often ignored. A useful overview of these schemes is provided by Bean and Melville.

The British government has acknowledged that they were mis-guided, and has established the Child Migrant Central Index to help migrants wishing to re-establish contact with their families. The index is intended to act as a signpost to the records of sending agencies; however, access is restricted to migrants and close relatives. Enquiries about the index should be made to the National Council of Voluntary Child Care Organisations, Unit 4, Pride Court, 80-82, White Lion Street, London N1 9PF. The website is **www.voluntarychild.org**

Prior to 1972, the Home Office had responsibility for government policy towards child migrants, and many relevant papers may be found in the National Archives, class MH102. These are mainly policy papers, and include information on emigration schemes such as those organized by Dr. Barnardo's Homes, the Fairbridge Society, the Overseas Migration Board, and Big Brother.

The Second World War prompted the establishment of the Childrens Overseas Reception Board, which operated between 1940 and 1944, and organized the evacuation of 3,100 children to the Dominions in 1940. Its records are in the National Archives (DO131) and includes registers of child applicants, with a small selection of case files.

After the war, a similar number of children were sent to Australia between 1947 and 1953 under approved emigration schemes. Records relating to them are held in various state archives in Australia. The Child Migrants Trust, 228, Canning Street, North Carlton, Victoria, 3054, Australia, is able to assist in tracing the records of both these and other children who emigrated from Britain in the twentieth century. Basic information about child migrants to Australia between 1913 and 1968 is also provided by the Western Australian Referral Index.

Canada was another major destination of child emigrants: over 100,000 migrated between 1870 and the 1940. Their names are being indexed at **www.archives.ca**

Soldiers formed another important category of emigrants. The Empire Settlement Act of 1922 offered free passage to de-mobilized soldiers, and 40,000 emigrated, mainly to Canada. Some policy records survive in the National Archives, but most information relating to these men will be in the archives of the receiving countries.

The second world war prompted another wave of emigration – perhaps 80,000 brides of American and Canadian servicemen, together with their babies. TRACE (the Transatlantic Childrens Enterprise) is a self-help support group for those seeking to trace their families.

Web Pages:

- Emigrants
  catalogue.pro.gov.uk/Leaflets/ri2272

- United Kingdom and Ireland: Emigration and Immigration
  www.genuki.org.uk/big/Emigration.html

- Passport Records
  catalogue.pro.gov.uk/Leaflets/ri2167.htm

- Passenger Lists
  catalogue.pro.gov.uk/Leaflets/ri2163.htm

- The Ships List
  www.theshipslist.com/

- Immigrant Ships Transcribers Guild
  istg.rootsweb.com

- Ellis Island On-Line
  www.ellisislandrecords.org/

- Ships Passenger Lists: Hugh Reekie's Index of Indexes
  members.attcanada.ca.~max-com/Ships.html

- Immigration Records (ship passenger arrival records)
  www.archives.gov/research__room/genealogy/ immigrant__arrivals/passenger__records.html
  At the U.S. National Archives & Records Administration

- Passenger Records held in Canberra
  **www.naa.gov.au/publications/fact__sheets/
  fs38.html**
  At the Australian Archives

- Passenger Lists 1865-1935
  www.archives.ca/02/020202/0202020401__e.html
  Held by the National Archives of Canada

- British Home Children
  **freepages.genealogy.rootsweb.com/
  ~britishhomechildren**

- Home Children
  **www.archives.ca/02/020202/
  0202020409__e.html**
  Sent to Canada

- TRACE: Transatlantic Children's Enterprise
  freespace.virgin.net/j.munro.trace.htm
  Helps trace GI families of World War II

Further Reading:

- KERSHAW, ROGER. *Emigrants and expats: a guide to sources on U.K. emigration and residents overseas.* Public Record Office readers guide **20**. 2002
- YEO, GEOFFREY. *The British overseas: a guide to records of their baptisms, births, marriages, deaths and burials avaialable in the United Kingdom.* 3rd ed. Guildhall Library, 1994.
- BEAN, P., & MELVILLE, J. *Lost children of the Empire.* Unwin Hyman, 1989.

Australia

- VINE HALL, NICK. *Tracing your family history in Australia: a guide to sources.* 3rd ed. Albert Park: N.Vine Hall, 2002.

Canada

- BAXTER, ANGUS. *In search of your Canadian roots: tracing your family tree in Canada.* 3rd ed. Baltimore: Genealogical Publishing, 2000.

New Zealand

- BROMELL, ANNE. *Tracing family history in New Zealand.* Godwit, 1996.

United States

- EAKLE, A., & CERNY, J. *The source: a guide book of American genealogy,* ed. Loretto Dennis Szucs & Sandra Hargreaves Luebking. Rev. ed. Salt Lake City: Ancestry Publishing, 1996.

Chapter 22

Miscellaneous Sources

Records of the Poor Law

'The existing poor law shall cease to have effect'. That announcement in the 1948 National Assistance Act finally ended the operation of the New Poor Law Act of 1834, under which paupers had been relieved for over 100 years. Its importance had, however, been considerably eroded since the law was originally enacted. School boards had assumed responsibilty for the education of the poor in the late nineteenth century; the old age pension was introduced in 1908; labour exchanges in 1909, health insurance in 1911. Guardians continued to function until 1930.

The records of the poor law are voluminous, including registers of workhouse births and deaths, admission and discharge registers, vaccination registers, lists of children boarded out, out-relief books, *etc., etc.* A full list, running to 4 pages, is given by Gibson, et al, who also provides a detailed listing of surviving archives. It is possible that some of these records will be closed to public access for up to 100 years. Most of the records of use to family historians will be found in county record offices; however, registers of staff prior to 1921 are in the

National Archives, class MH9. Personal details can also be found in returns made to Parliament by Poor Law Union officials; these are in the Parliamentary papers (see chapter 17).

Further Reading:

- FOWLER, SIMON. *Using poor law records.* Public Record Office, 2001.
- GIBSON, JEREMY. et al. *Poor Law Union records.* 2nd ed. 4 vols. F.F.H.S., 1997-2000.
- REID, ANDY. *The Union Workhouse: a study guide for teachers and local historians.* Learning local history 3. Phillimore for the British Association for Local History, 1994.

Estate Records

Title deeds and other estate records – leases, rentals, surveys, *etc.* – are invaluable sources for family historians. They may enable you to date your ancestor's occupation of a particular property, and may provide details of his tenancy. Unfortunately; they are less likely to be available for the twentieth century than for previous periods. The progressive introduction of compulsory land registration between 1862 and 1990 ended the need to retain old title deeds, and many have been destroyed. Many more are likely to be still held in solicitors offices, or in the possession of landowners themselves. The small number of manorial court rolls which continued until copyhold tenure was abolished in 1925 are, however, easily found: they should be listed in the Historical

Manuscripts Commission Manorial Documents register, which also lists a wide range of other early twentieth century manorial documents.

The Land Registry records are not of much help to the genealogist. Its register now covers a major proportion of property, but it only includes details of current owners, together with maps or plans of properties. It is unable to help with genealogical inquiries.

Web Page:

- Manorial Documents Register
  www.hmc.gov.uk/mdr/mdr.htm

- H.M. Land Registry
  www.landreg.gov.uk

World Wars I & II

The two world wars, both of which required the mobilisation of the entire population, generated an enormous amount of paper, much of which survives in the National Archives and in county record offices. Records relating to the army, and to the national farm survey (see chapters 12 & 19) have already been discussed, but these are merely the tip of the iceberg. A.R.P. wardens, the evacuation of children, war damage claims, invasion defence plans, munitions workers: these are just a few of the subjects which are covered in the archives, and which may contain information of value to the family historian.

Unfortunately, there is no overall survey of these

sources from the point of view of the family historian. The works by Beckett and Cantwell provide details listings of records in the National Archives, but hide much material of value by their uninformative descriptions, which rarely indicate that family historians may be interested in particular classes. Creaton's book is much more useful; it is a comprehensive discussion of all surviving sources for second world war London, many of which may be replicated in other areas. Hall's survey is now somewhat dated, but worth a read, and includes a useful listing of local war records (although locations given will have changed).

Further Reading:

- BECKETT, IAN F.W. *The First World War: the essential guide to sources in the U.K. national archives.* Public Record Office, 2002.
- CANTWELL, JOHN D. *The Second World War: a guide to documents in the Public Record Office.* 2nd ed. Public Record Office handbooks 15. H.M.S.O. 1993.
- CREATON, HEATHER. *Sources for the history of London 1939-45: a guide and bibliography.* Archives and the user 9. British Records Association, 1998.
- MAYOR, SYDNEY L., & KOENIG, WILLIAM J. *The two world wars: a guide to manuscript collections in the U.K.* New York: Bowker, 1976.
- HALL, HUBERT. *British archives and the sources for the history of the world war.* Oxford University Press, 1925.

Family Histories, Pedigrees & Biographies

Has it been done before? Innumerable family histories and pedigrees have been compiled, and biographies are one of the most popular forms of light reading. Such works have an obvious importance for the family historian; if they are available, then you obviously need to know about them. Quite apart from their intrinsic interest for family members, it is likely that family histories in particular will include pedigrees and details of sources consulted. Biographies may also include a pedigree, and will almost certainly give details of close family. It is also worth finding out about works on other families who may have lived in the same areas as your ancestors; they may provide relevant information.

You may think it unlikely that there are any such works relating to your family. It is, however, always worth checking bibliographies and library catalogues for any that may have escaped your attention. The British Library holds an extensive collection of biographies and family histories; its catalogue is readily available on the internet, and printed catalogues of the British Museum (the British Library's predecessor) are available in most major reference libraries. The county volumes of Raymond's *British genealogical library guides* provide extensive listings of family histories and pedigrees; biographies are listed at length in McColvin's bibliography and also in the *Bibliography of biography.* The many brief accounts of family history research printed in the journals of family history societies also ought to be checked; they are listed in the digest section of the Federation of Family History Societies journal, *Family history news & digest.* Raymond's county guides, where they are available, also list them.

Most entries in biographical dictionaries are also likely to include details of parentage, spouse(s) and children. An extraordinarily wide range of such dictionaries is available; over 16,000 are listed in Slocum, and over 3,000,000 entries are indexed in the *Biography and genealogy master index.* The *Dictionary of national biography, Who's who,* and *Who was who* are the best known of such compilations, and are widely available in libraries, but there are also many others relating to specific groups of people. Some of those relating to particular occupations have already been discussed (above, p. 69). Many relating to particular counties were published in the early years of this century, and are listed by Hanham.

Further Reading:

- RAYMOND, STUART A. *British genealogical library guides.* F.F.H.S., 1988- . See especially the county volumes, some of which are solely devoted to family histories.
- McCOLVIN, L. R. *The librarian's subject guide to books. Vol.2. Biography, family history, genealogy, etc.* James Clarke & Co., 1960.
- *Bibliography of biography 1970-1984.* 40 fiche. British Library, 1985.

- SLOCUM, R. B. *Biographical dictionaries and related works: an international bibliography ...* 2nd ed. Gale Research, 1986.
- *Biography and genealogy master index: a consolidated index to more than 3,200,000 biographical sketches in over 350 current and retrospective biographical dictionaries.* 8 vols. Gale, 1980. Supplements 1981-5, 1986-9, and annually from 1990. Also available on CD.
- HANHAM, H. J. 'Neglected sources of biographical information: county biographical dictionaries, 1890-1937', *Bulletin of the Institute of Historical Research* **34**(89), 1961, 55-66.

Appendix

Addresses

Most addresses of institutions have been given in the body of the text above. Those which have been mentioned repeatedly, or are generally important, are listed here.

Society of Genealogists
14 Charterhouse Buildings
London
EC1M 7BA

www.sog.org.uk

Federation of Family History Societies
P.O.Box 2425
Coventry CV5 6XX

www.ffhs.org.uk

Guild of One Name Studies
Box G,
14, Charterhouse Buildings,
Goswell Road
London, EC1M 7BA

www.one-name.org/intro.html

National Archives
Ruskin Avenue
Kew, Richmond
Surrey, TW9 4DU

www.pro.gov.uk

Family Records Centre
1 Myddleton Street
London, EC1R 1UW

www.familyrecords.gov.uk/frc/default.htm

British Library
96 Euston Road
London, NW1 2DB

www.bl.uk

Historical Manuscripts Commission
Quality House
Quality Court
Chancery Lane
London, WC2A 1HP

www.hmc.gov.uk

Guildhall Library
Aldermanbury
London, EC2

www.ihrinfo.ac.uk/gh/

Index